Praise for *Big Fat Lies Women Tell Themselves*

"A must-read for any woman who is sick and tired of being so darn hard on herself. Like a doctor of self-love, Amy Ahlers delivers powerful prescriptions that do more than soothe the symptoms. She takes you to the root and masterfully shows you how to make change that lasts!"

— Christine Arylo, author of *Choosing ME before WE*

"This book...will supercharge your life! [It] provides true solutions and spiritual nourishment and shows you how to use the power of your Inner Wisdom and your awakened Inner Superstar."

— from the foreword by SARK, artist and author of
Glad No Matter What

"Stop everything you are doing — you have to read this book! I was blown away by the powerful content in *Big Fat Lies Women Tell Themselves* and completely inspired by the clear and effective direction that Amy Ahlers provides. This is the book that you pass on to your closest girlfriend or daughter when she needs to be reminded of her greatness."

— Lisa Nichols, author of *No Matter What!*

"In a refreshingly disarming tone, Amy Ahlers helps women pierce the veil of deception that keeps us from discovering our greatest selves. *Big Fat Lies Women Tell Themselves* is packed full of real truth and wisdom. I highly recommend this book for any woman who just wants to be happy."

— Kristine Carlson, author of
Don't Sweat the Small Stuff for Women

"In *Big Fat Lies Women Tell Themselves*, Amy Ahlers shines light on the destructive stories women choose to believe. This timely book will transform your fear-based illusions into miracles and reconnect you with your loving truth. With Amy as your guide, you are destined to awaken your Inner Superstar!"

— Gabrielle Bernstein, bestselling author of
Add More ~ing to Your Life and *Spirit Junkie*

BIG FAT
LIES
WOMEN TELL
THEMSELVES

BIG FAT LIES

WOMEN TELL THEMSELVES

Ditch Your Inner Critic and
Wake Up Your Inner Superstar

Amy Ahlers

Foreword by SARK

New World Library
Novato, California

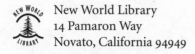
New World Library
14 Pamaron Way
Novato, California 94949

Image on page 130 from *The Money Keys* by Karen Russo © 2007 Karen Russo. Used with permission.
Authenticity self-assessment questionnaire on pages 178–80 © Rich Rusdorf, CPCC. Used with permission.

Text design by Tona Pearce Myers

Library of Congress Cataloging-in-Publication Data
Ahlers, Amy.
Big fat lies women tell themselves : ditch your inner critic and wake up your inner superstar / Amy Ahlers.
     p. cm.
ISBN 978-1-60868-028-3 (pbk.)
1. Women—Psychology. 2. Self-esteem in women. 3. Life skills.
4. Self-confidence. I. Title.
HQ1206.A28 2011
155.3'332—dc23   2011028704

First printing, October 2011
ISBN 978-1-60868-028-3
Printed in Canada on 100% postconsumer-waste recycled paper

 New World Library is a proud member of the Green Press Initiative.

10 9 8 7 6 5 4 3 2

For my daughter, Annabella, whose Inner Superstar shines oh-so-bright. May you always feel deeply connected to your light and the truth of how magnificent you are. You are loved.

And for Rob, who loves me in my moments of brilliance and my moments of darkness. Thank you for showing me how to unconditionally love.

Contents

Big Fat Lies about Body and Self-Care

Big Fat Lies about Success

Big Fat Lies about Money

Big Fat Lies about Love and Relationships

foreword
By SARK

I deeply know the pain of living with big inner lies and negative self-talk. I now know the profound liberation and power of living differently.

We are all conditioned to believe these kinds of lies from an early age, and most of us continue this way for a lifetime. Amy's beautifull book shines a big, bold light on the big fat lies we tell ourselves and shows us how to change our inner dialogue, empower our Inner Wisdom, and wake up our Inner Superstar.

Take a tour through the fifty-nine lies in this book, and you'll recognize yourself, or perhaps your best friend, sister, mother, or daughter. Read and absorb the "truths" and let them illuminate and change you. Explore and practice with the "challenges" and allow them to transform you. Use the "affirmations" to support your new beliefs.

In my more than twenty years of writing transformative books and teaching life-changing workshops, I have never encountered anything more detrimental than believing the kind of lies we tell ourselves, then living out the results of thinking that way. Lack of self-love and self-worth is a profound epidemic passed on through the generations, unless people are shown how to live differently.

This book does just that. In practical and accessible language, it shows you how to think and live differently. And Amy doesn't just expose the lies—she reveals the masks they might be wearing. Trust me: these will feel familiar to you too. She also provides real-life examples, both from her own life and from the lives of people remarkably like you.

Good news! You are definitely not the only one, and in fact, you are in excellent company. I would also like to note that Amy Ahlers walks her talk or "runs her buns" with the processes in this book. I know this because we are both personally and professionally connected, and I've witnessed her practicing and experienced her first-rate coaching. I can

Also tell you that she's an outstanding mom to her daughter, AnnABella.

This book provides true solutions and spiritual nourishment and shows you how to use the power of your Inner Wisdom and your Awakened Inner Superstar. You'll also learn an extremely effective three-step process to use anytime to disengage from your Inner Critics and to empower yourself to make significant changes and see the growth in your life.

This book, including the wonderful list of resources at the back, will supercharge your life!

Susan Ariel Rainbow Kennedy AKA SARK
GLAD NO MATTER WHAT: Transforming Loss and Change into Gift and Opportunity
planetSARK.com

Introduction

The most important relationship in your life is your rela-tionship with you. And most of us are not doing so hot. We are incredibly, intensely hard on ourselves. And that stinks.

We think that if we were just accomplished enough, thin enough, beautiful enough, rich enough, we could then magically shift our internal dialogue into an empowering, nurturing, loving one. But after more than a decade of coaching women from every conceivable walk of life, I finally got it: women are really hard on themselves *despite* their external circumstances. We all engage in beat-ing ourselves up both for the big things and for the tiniest imperfections. And it isn't helping us to become more successful or to feel more fulfilled or even to get more done.

> *The most important relationship in your life is your relationship with YOU.*

And who can blame us for being so hard on ourselves? We

have a lot on our plates: careers, romance, kids, health...the list goes on and on. We're supposed to bring home the bacon, fry it up in a pan, have incredible sex with our partners (never letting him forget he's a man — that is, assuming he is a man), get the laundry and housework done, have healthy, accomplished kids and a tight ass and perky boobs to boot. We begin to feel like we're supposed to enjoy being pulled in a million directions at the same time. And that we're supposed to be as flexible as Gumby on muscle relaxers. But we're only human. How about we give ourselves a break?

The Cost of Our Lies

The National Science Foundation has discovered that the average person thinks as many as sixty thousand thoughts a day and that the vast majority of them are negative and critical. In other words, we're telling ourselves Big Fat Lies over and over again until we become addicted to them. This internal battle eats away at self-love, self-worth, and self-esteem, leading to depression, dissatisfaction, decreased productivity, and heart-stopping stress.

We're paying a high price for these Lies. Here are some facts for those of you who are statistic junkies:

- We're stressed out, and the National Institute of Health reports that 70 percent of all disease is stress related.
- We're worried. *Time* magazine has proclaimed that women are more powerful, but less happy, than they've ever been.
- Even when we're doing well, we don't *feel* as if we're doing well. According to Betsey Stevenson and Justin Wolfers in "The Paradox of Declining Female Happiness," "By many objective measures the lives of women in the United States have improved over the past thirty-five

years, yet we show that measures of subjective well-being indicate that women's happiness has declined both absolutely and relative to men."

- And all this self-loathing is seriously affecting our mental health. The National Institutes of Mental Health report that nearly *twice as many American women* as men are affected by depression and that between five and ten million women and girls suffer from eating disorders.

How depressing is *that*? I mean, it wasn't so long ago that women were banding together to win the right to vote, and now here we are powerful and free...and totally miserable. It's time for us to fling open our windows and yell, "I'm mad as hell and I'm not going to take it anymore!" (Thank you, Paddy Chayefsky.) I know it and you know it; we are ready to get our happiness on — and not just by popping a pill. It is high time we went easy on ourselves, just for the sheer joy of it. Are you ready? Let me show you how.

> *Don't believe everything you think.*

The Inner Critic

Allow me to introduce you to your Inner Critic, or Inner Mean Girl, a term coined by my colleague Christine Arylo and me. Your Inner Mean Girl is negative. She's catty. She's judgmental.

She compares your worst to everyone else's best. In her eyes, you lose every time.

She spews cruel words at you and makes you feel like you're in seventh grade again — and *not* in the popular group. Your Inner Mean Girl's favorite thing to do is to make you feel small, inadequate, and unworthy. She's always finding evidence to prove her theory: *you are not enough.*

Well, I've got news for you: Your Inner Critic is a Big Fat

Liar! She tells you Big Fat Lies to try to maintain the status quo and keep you in your comfort zones. Even if your comfort zones aren't all that comfortable. She will tell you over and over that "you're not enough," "it's too late," and "you're a failure."

All Lies.

Once you realize that your Inner Critic is a liar, see if you can't catch her in the act. (Hint: Whenever you're feeling bad about yourself, she's right there with a megaphone.) Notice how she loves to speak in absolutes. She uses words like *never, always, forever, all, everybody, must, nothing,* and *no one* to punish you and make you feel like a lost cause. She sees things only in black and white, leaving no room for being human.

Think you're alone? Think only obviously insecure women believe these Lies or let their Inner Critics run the show? Think again! When we hear powerhouses such as Elizabeth Gilbert, bestselling author of *Eat, Pray Love*, declare, "Despite having written five books, I worry that I have not written the right *kinds* of books" or Oprah admitting to the world that her focus on her weight has robbed her of joy: "I'm mad at myself. I'm embarrassed. I can't believe that after all these years, all the things I know how to do, I'm still talking about my weight," we realize that the Inner Mean Girl, and her Big Fat Lies, is omnipresent among even the most successful women. In other words, this is *not* a personal failure.

Get to Know *Your* Inner Critic's Big Fat Lies

I've been speaking, teaching, and leading courses alongside Inner Mean Girl Reform School cocreator, Christine Arylo, about the Inner Mean Girl and her Big Fat Lies. (And I've created a free reader's tool kit at www.BigFatLiesTheBook.com, where you'll receive a complimentary Inner Mean Girl Transformation Kit. Please go there right now to get yours!) After coaching thousands of women, I have learned the Inner Mean Girl can show up in many different forms. For some of you, she might feel more like an Inner Sad Girl or an Inner Rageaholic or an Inner Pollyanna. However she shows up for you, I want to help you get to know your Inner Mean Girl so that you can banish her once and for all!

Begin by considering the following:

- Identify your Inner Critic's Top 10 List of places, situations, and environments where she likes to show up and criticize. Is it at work? Social events? In bed? Whenever you look in the mirror? Once you know what circumstances are likely to trigger the Inner Critic, you can be better prepared to deal with her.

- Next, draw a picture of your Inner Critic. Is she fat with big glasses? Perfectly pressed in pink? A slob with a cigarette in one hand and a martini in the other? Don't worry if you think you can't draw. No one will ever see this but you, so go for it! And if you really don't want to draw, you can find an image in a magazine or on the Internet that captures your Inner Mean Girl. It is helpful to have a mental image of the voice that tortures you.

- Get to know your Inner Mean Girl on a deeper level. Notice what makes her louder, and notice what diminishes her power. What happens if you just yell "Shut up!" at her? What if you just look her calmly in the eye and reassure her that everything is going to be all right? Maybe she needs a compliment every now and then. After all, Inner Critics need love too.

- What are your Inner Critic's favorite Big Fat Lies? What does she say to you over and over? (Hint: Use the table of contents of this book if you need some examples.) Your Inner Mean Girl will collect evidence to make her case. She'll do everything she can to back up her favorite punishing, disappointing, sad stories about you and your worth.

Signs That You Are Letting Your Inner Critic Run the Show

The presence of any of these painful emotions is a clear sign that you have fallen for your Inner Mean Girl's Big Fat Lies:

- fear
- hopelessness
- insecurity/unworthiness
- depression
- guilt
- regret
- anger
- blame
- boredom
- pessimism
- frustration
- impatience
- disappointment
- jealousy

Are you getting how crazy-making it is to believe her Lies? Now that you've become aware of your Inner Critic and the stories she tells, it's time to tune in to that other voice inside you — the voice of your Inner Wisdom.

Get to Know Your Inner Wisdom

I've got some great news for you: as loud and nasty as the voice of your Inner Critic can be, another voice inside you is even more powerful: the voice of your Truth, which I like to call your Inner Wisdom. Take a moment right now and tune in to your Inner Wisdom. Close your eyes, take a deep breath, and invite her in. Feel her deep inside you, beckoning you to wake up to your magnificence.

Recall a time when your Inner Wisdom was 100 percent present. A time when you just knew something was right for you or that a certain someone was bad news. Maybe you followed your Inner Wisdom's voice, and sure enough, your intuition was right on. Or perhaps you went against your gut instinct and regretted it later, exclaiming to your best friend, "I *knew* I shouldn't have gone on that date!" or "I could just feel this wasn't the right job for me, and I took it anyway." Maybe your Inner Wisdom shows up when you are cooking, painting, hiking, taking a long bath, or writing — you know, the times when you just feel divinely guided. (Want some help accessing your Inner Wisdom? I've created an MP3 of a guided visualization just for you. Go to www.BigFatLiesTheBook .com to grab that, as well as a whole tool kit of other fun extras.)

Allow your Inner Wisdom to bubble up. Let's really connect with her so you can get to know her better. Begin with the following:

- Notice how your Inner Wisdom communicates with you. Does she whisper in your ear? Do you feel her in your body? Do you see images before your eyes? Or perhaps you just *know* when she's there? Become aware of how she connects with you.

- Draw a picture of your Inner Wisdom. What is her essence? Feel free to grab paints, crayons, or pencils to sketch away. Or maybe get an image off the Internet or do a collage. Let's get her really present.

- Allow your Inner Wisdom to respond to your Inner Critic's Biggest Fattest Lies. If you ask and remain open, you'll be able to know/hear/see/feel her responses. By the way, your Inner Wisdom can also tell you some hard truths, but she does it from love and compassion, as opposed to shame and judgment.

Great job! Doesn't it feel downright yummy to lean into your Inner Wisdom? You know you are focusing on your Inner Wisdom's truth when you feel:

- joy
- laughter
- happiness
- optimism
- a sense of fun and adventure
- inspiration
- freedom
- empowerment
- enthusiasm
- passion
- hope
- groundedness
- knowing

I highly recommend creating space each day to connect with your Inner Wisdom. You may feel her most strongly when you are in prayer or meditation, which can include anything from sitting in silence to listening to a chant to reading from a meditation book. You might also want to make a habit of checking in with her before any new decision or endeavor. Maybe you can keep an image or icon of her near your work station, next to your bed, or even in your car. Some women invoke their Inner Wisdom as they put on lotion each morning, so they can get dressed feeling blessed by their true selves. Others take a moment before making an important phone call or sending an email. I have a mindfulness bell that I keep running in the background on my computer that rings every seventy-five minutes when I'm working to remind me to connect to my Inner Wisdom, breathe, and stretch! Whatever way *feels* right to you to bring your Inner Wisdom into the daily warp and weft of your life *is* right. Keep exploring — there's no end to the gifts your

Inner Wisdom wants to share with you. You'll be amazed at how wise she is!

Waking Up Your Inner Superstar

As you connect more and more to your Inner Wisdom, you'll begin to feel your light shining brighter. Remember the song that goes "This little light of mine, I'm gonna let it shine"? That's exactly what you're doing: remembering how to let your light shine. When you wake up your Inner Superstar, your radiance and light will shine more brightly than it ever has before.

I want you to feel so connected to your Inner Wisdom, to your source energy, to God, to the universe, to the Divine, to the light inside you that you cannot help but become your Inner Superstar. When you fully wake up to your Inner Superstar, you make heads turn as you walk into a room because you are so deeply and fully being *you*. You are in the flow. You become a magnet for everything your heart desires because you are like a beacon of happiness, love, and success.

We've all had moments of feeling this connection to our Inner Superstar, and I'm here to tell you that you can *live* from this place, that it can become your new comfort zone. You can feel like shining bright is your new home. When you disarm your Inner Critic and your Inner Mean Girl, you become so aligned with the truth of who you really are that your light becomes undeniable. That is what this book is about, unleashing your Inner Superstar and waking her up in your life. I'll give you the tools to rouse her and keep her awake so you can always be in tune with your grace and inner beauty. It's time to shine!

Here's the Truth That I Know about You…

You are brilliant…and when you're not, it is because you are disconnected from your Inner Superstar. You are loving and ready to be loved…and when you're not, it is because you are

9

disconnected from your Inner Superstar. You are kind...and when you're not, it is because you are disconnected from your Inner Superstar.

Find the truth of how powerful you are.

When you're disconnected from your Inner Superstar, you are disconnected from your Truth, from your Inner Wisdom, from the part of you that is deeply and fully connected to your source energy. In other words, you've unplugged yourself from the Divine or however you refer to a higher power. Perhaps the universe? Collective consciousness? Life force? God? Jesus? Buddha? It's time for you to unleash your Inner Wisdom and let your Inner Superstar lead.

The Choice Is Yours

As you dive into this book and begin to change the way you think and act, you may be tempted to go back to life as usual. It's called homeostasis: our minds, bodies, and spirits tend to go back to what we know. We slip back to our to-do lists, our everyday existence. We go back to the life we know and our habits. We ignore our opportunities for transformation. At each moment, you are at a choice point:

You can choose a perspective that makes you feel bad and thus more prone to believing your Inner Critic and her Big Fat Lies.

or

You can choose a perspective that makes you feel good, thus bringing you to the path of Truth and aligning you with your Inner Wisdom. This path will lead you to more happiness and success in all areas of your life. It will allow you to fully wake up your Inner Superstar.

The choice is yours.

So now consider me your coach and your personal wake-up call. I am conspiring with your Inner Wisdom and your Inner Superstar to help you realize how truly fabulous you are. I invite you to stop the Lies that run rampant in your life so that you can live your dreams and experience more joy. I invite you to take your power back from your Inner Mean Girl and to shine bright!

The Wake-Up Call Three-Step Process

You may be thinking, "Amy, how do I do that? How do I choose to wake up my Inner Superstar?" This book is filled with transformational tools to help you whenever specific Big Fat Lies come up. And I have a powerful process that I've developed over the last eleven years that is the foundational go-to tool at any time. Whenever you feel any painful emotions or the presence of your Inner Mean Girl, take yourself through this three-step process:

- *Step One:* Ask yourself, "What is my Inner Mean Girl saying?" Really articulate that voice. 'Fess up to the ugly, sad words that are clanging around in your head. Often just hearing the words aloud will wake you up and shake you out of your emotional slump. Bring the Big Fat Lies out of the darkness and into the light so they can be healed.
- *Step Two:* Close your eyes, take a deep breath, and ask yourself, "What does my Inner Wisdom know?" And then let her speak — not platitudes or forced optimism but rather the Truth about who you are and what your soul's purpose might be in this moment.
- *Step Three:* Finally, let your Inner Wisdom's Truth take root by repeating it back (aloud if possible), accompanied

by a physical gesture to really lock in the message. This is a potent neuro-linguistic programming (NLP) technique to bring your physical body into alignment with your Truth. My Inner Wisdom has me tap my heart, my client Jeanine waves her hand like a butterfly floating away from her, and my friend Alison touches her belly. Attaching a physical gesture not only deepens the learning, but it also gives you a movement to engage in whenever you are feeling angry, upset, or sad. Your Inner Wisdom's gesture will remind your body to calm down, even without words.

For example, let's say that you are overweight and are beating yourself up about it. You could begin to believe your Inner Mean Girl and buy into her Lies, such as "I am fat and I'll never get this under control" or "I'm worthless." Or, you could choose to believe your Inner Wisdom's Truth, one filled with self-compassion and desire: "I've had a lot on my plate and I've let my weight slip, and I believe in my power to get back on track" and "I am ready and committed to carving out time for self-care." Shift your focus to your Inner Wisdom; it will always bring you in line with your Truth and compassion, and you will always feel better. As you practice this process more and more, you'll find that you are stirring your Inner Superstar to life.

Why Do We Lie?

As you read this, you may find yourself asking, "Why the Lies? Why are women so hard on themselves? Why do we let our Inner Critics have all the power?" Through my personal experience and my work as a coach, I've found it's because human beings feel more comfortable "playing small." We cling to comfort, thus continuing to hold our own power hostage. We feel terrified that we might be put in our place and as a result stay in the jail cell we know and understand. Our power as women is deep and vast and in many ways more mysterious than the "he-man" masculine form of power we've been indoctrinated with since we were little girls. As we learn to love and embrace our Inner Wisdom and Inner Superstar, we will become more comfortable with our own magnificence and authority. And as we shine ever brighter, we will witness others learning to shine. What a beautiful world it would be if we all stood tall and proud and compassionate and vital and wise and loving, confident in ourselves and in one another. We can relish our strength and the awesome responsibility it carries to be in service to ourselves, one another, and the world, instead of hiding from it.

Stop lying!
Choose the truth.
Feel great.

Take a minute to imagine feeling powerful and happy. Imagine a world in which every woman feels powerful and happy. Is it scary or uncomfortable? If so, that discomfort may be the very reason you tell yourself these Lies.

As you work your way through this program and unravel your Inner Mean Girl's Lies, it is essential to look for the payoff of each of your Lies. After all, there is always some sort of payoff — otherwise, we wouldn't be telling ourselves Big Fat Lies! Common payoffs include:

- Getting to be right — "I knew it wouldn't work!"
- Taking yourself out of the game before someone else can — "I failed the exam because I didn't study."
- Feeling included in a group — "We *all* complain about our marriages!"
- Not having to claim your power — "I can't do anything about it."

- Maintaining comfort and familiarity — "I better not rock the boat."
- Getting attention — "I need help!"
- Feeling justified — "I'm upset, so it's okay to have a cookie."
- Clinging to anger and blame — "I'll never forgive that person."

Understanding the payoff of your Lies can help you unravel the web of self-deception and get your power back. Notice which of the payoffs above most resonate with you, pay attention to when that feeling comes up, and ask yourself, "What is the Truth?" or "What does my Inner Wisdom know?"

Operation Manual

The structure of *Big Fat Lies Women Tell Themselves* is simple and accessible. Each Lie is accompanied by:

- *The Truth*: a wake-up call and real-life example to inspire you to break through your negative thinking with positive, empowering thoughts and perspectives.
- *Challenge*: a practical coaching exercise that allows you to put the Truth into action. I highly encourage you to complete the exercises outlined in the challenges. Write, doodle, and draw your way to your Inner Wisdom. I've created some handy-dandy worksheets and affirmations for you to download and print out at www .BigFatLiesTheBook.com if you prefer to write your work separately. Why not create a Big Fat Lies folder or binder?
- *Affirmation*: a mantra you can repeat aloud to cement your new learning. In my online tool kit you'll also find

printable affirmations to put on your mirror or dash-board. This will be an easy reminder of the Truth about how fabulous you are!

• Finally, you'll find an inspiring quotation to motivate and encourage you.

Consider this book a joyous, straight-talking Cracker Jack box of treats with the best possible prize inside: a better life. *Big Fat Lies* is an easy-to-follow path to personal transformation. After all, we're a culture of fast food, fast talk, fast Internet, fast planes, trains, and automobiles. How about some *fast self-help*?

You may choose to use this book in several different ways:

• Read the entire book, marking the Lies that you wish to work on and come back to.

• Each week read and put into practice one section of Big Fat Lies.

• Use the book as a regular meditation tool-for-truth. Simply pick up the book whenever you think of it, flip to a Lie/Truth, and notice how a seemingly random flip of the pages can take you closer to your Truth.

You Are Doing Affirmations All the Time

Let's *talk* affirmations! Here's the truth: we are doing affirmations all the time…whether or not we know it. It's just that we're usually doing negative affirmations that we've *unconsciously* programmed. In other words, we are usually affirming Big Fat Lies. After all, beliefs are just thoughts you've had over and over. So throughout this book, I invite you to create positive affirmations and to change your thought patterns. I promise you that if you do the work and affirm your truths daily, you'll change the way you think. And that, my dear one, is life changing!

Are You Ready?

Finally, since I consider you a new girlfriend, get ready to hear stories from my own life, my friends' lives, my colleagues' lives, and my clients' lives (all identifying characteristics and names of clients have been changed to protect their privacy, of course). I've learned so much from so many people, and you're just going to love getting to know some of the inspiring people I've been fortunate enough to encounter on my life path.

Whatever way you choose to use this book, I hope that you find it enlightening and useful. I recognize that *you* are the expert on your own life. You are the only one living *your* life and the only one who knows the truth of your relationship with yourself, so allow these words to wash over you and inspire you so you can wake you up to your Inner Superstar.

And now, on to the Big Fat Lies....

The Mother Lode:

BIG FAT LIES ABOUT YOUR WORTH

I call the *Big Fat Lies* about yourself and the world at large
the mother lode. These are the foundational Big Fat Lies that
you've built your life on. These negative thoughts come up over
and over, torturing you daily. They are the Big Fat Lies that ap-
pear as core truths, when in reality, they are simply *your story*
about life.

You may even know on a rational level that these Big Fat Lies
aren't true. But still they creep up through your cells, through
your subconscious mind, fueling your Inner Mean Girl. And then
suddenly, you feel like the wind got knocked out of you.

Our mission in this section of the book is to uncover the biggest, fattest foundational Lie that you find yourself believing. I
want you to hit the mother lode! And then let's transform that Lie
into a Truth that you can take to the bank, so that you'll have a
new golden Truth your Inner Superstar will be able to cash in on.
This new Truth will transform your relationship with yourself
into a loving, nurturing, positive, and healthy one.

Now, you may be thinking, "Amy, is this just about blowing
sunshine up my booty and filling up my ego?" *No!* Your Inner
Wisdom and Inner Superstar's job is not just to tell you what a
gorgeous-fabulous-badass you are (although we *love* it when she
says that!). I'm not asking you to become Stuart Smalley from
the *Saturday Night Live* sketch looking in the mirror saying, "And
gosh darn it, people like me!" Your job is to create an honest relationship with yourself. So even though there may be moments
when you need to deliver a tough-love truth (e.g., "get out of this

relationship" or "honey, put the cookie down" or "it's time to get healthy and exercise, for goodness sake"), you'll be delivering that wake-up call Truth from a loving foundation. You need to know on a deep, core level that:

- You are enough.
- You are a good person.
- You are lovable.
- You belong.
- *Yes!* The universe is a friendly place.
- And more…

You must operate from a place of love and "enoughness"! It is high time you did a little spring cleaning on your Big Fat foundational Lies, a soul cleanse, if you will, so you can begin to see the truth of how fabulous you are. I want you to be as kind to yourself as you would be to your best friend or a newborn baby.

When I work with my coaching clients, we begin this exploration by getting curious about what they tell themselves when things go wrong. So think for a moment about the last time something went south. It could be a small thing or a big thing, from missing the subway to losing a loved one. What was the familiar, negative thought that raced through your mind? Was it "I'm not enough" or "I'm unlovable"? Perhaps you told yourself "I'm damaged goods" or "The world is against me." Ouch! You've just hit the mother lode Big Fat Lie for you.

In this section, you'll find challenge exercises to help you develop your self-worth, self-love, and self-esteem. Really, I want you to hold yourself in the highest esteem and operate from a deep level of self-respect. And don't be surprised if you need to come back to these exercises regularly. We're working on core beliefs here, so repetition is key.

Let's investigate these mother lode Lies one by one. Notice which Big Fat Lie is most familiar to you, and work on it until you start to transform. Ready, set, dig!

BIG FAT LIE #1

I am not enough.

Can also show up as:

I'm not good enough.
I'm worthless.

The Truth: An online survey conducted by Oprah.com asked readers, "What is missing in your life?" The number one answer by far was self-love. This Lie, the one that says you are not good enough, that you are not worthy, is pandemic, but don't believe it: you *are* good enough. You *do* add up. You *are* worthy. Declaring that you are enough is a decision. It's high time you decided that you are enough. It's a big decision to make, so don't worry if it takes practice. You will need to decide over and over *until it becomes your core belief.*

I recently co-led a three-day retreat alongside Christine Arylo, with our Inner Wisdom Golden Circle, twenty-one extraordinary women who have committed to creating a breakthrough in their lives. I was astonished by their vulnerability and by their bravery in telling the truth about how the "I am not enough" Big Fat Lie has sabotaged them repeatedly. We ended our weekend together with each woman standing strong in the middle of the circle, where we affirmed for her what she most needed to hear. The words *you are enough* were said over and over. I now invite you into the center of our virtual circle. Imagine yourself surrounded by a group of radiant women who love you for who you are. Imagine us saying to you, "You are enough." Let those words wash over you as you complete the challenge below.

Challenge: The series of questions and suggestions below will help you remember how much you love yourself and how "enough" you are:

- What is your inherent worth? Notice that the question isn't "What do you *do* that makes you worthy?" Start examining who you are *being* in the world. Make a list of the qualities that contribute to your inherent worth, and post it in a place where you will see it daily. Your inherent worth could include your positive attitude, your smile, the way you respect others, or the way you parent your child.
- Note the times when you consistently put your self-worth and self-love up for sale. Do certain people in your life create a sense of unworthiness? (When you visit your best friend from high school, do you feel like a loser? Do you feel unworthy after lunch with your negative coworker?) What instigates your feelings of self-loathing? (When you think of your body and how out of shape you are, do you begin to go to the "dark side"?)
- Make a commitment to be 100 percent conscious about the areas and people in your life that perpetuate feelings of unworthiness. Try to spend less time with "energy vampires" — you know, those negative people who seem to suck the energy and light right out of you. Or, if possible, drop relationships with those Negative Nellies altogether!

These feelings of unworthiness almost always stem from childhood. It's as if the kid or preteen in us is still screaming for approval and love. So let's reschool ourselves in a loving way with the following game. Our goal here is to replace feelings of unworthiness with self-love, self-acceptance, self-approval, and self-worth.

- Remember those gold star charts from grammar school? Let's create one that allows you to acknowledge how well you are taking care of yourself — it's your Inner Superstar Chart. Here's an example: My client Danielle was pretty, confident, and self-reliant, but whenever she got around her sisters she was reduced to a belligerent thirteen-year-old. She gave herself a gold star every time she kept her cool around her siblings' teasing (they thought they were being funny, but she always felt criticized).

- You get double gold stars when you maintain self-love in the most challenging areas and around the most challenging people. Danielle got a double gold star every time she remembered to leave the family gatherings before the heavy drinking and sappy storytelling began. You may want to give yourself stars every time you don't get sucked into a complaint session with your friend at work, or every time you say no to something you truly do not want to do (bake sale, anyone?). Remember, the goal here is to create mindfulness about those times when you tend to abandon yourself and to instead reward yourself for being on your own team.

- Treat yourself when you hit milestones. Danielle's system: ten stars equaled a walk on the beach, twenty stars equaled a trip to a massage therapist or nail salon, and one hundred stars equaled a vacation! Go on — I double-dog dare you!

Affirmation: All the gold stars in the world couldn't begin to convey my true worth!

> *"We often block our own blessings because we don't feel inherently good enough or smart enough or pretty enough or worthy enough… You're worthy because you are born and because you are here. Your being here, your being alive makes worthiness your birthright. You alone are enough."*

— OPRAH WINFREY, talk show host and self-made billionaire

I'm a total fraud.

Can also show up as:

I'm an imposter.

The Truth: Your Inner Critic loves to hook into this Lie when you are growing, stretching, and taking risks. Whenever you are out of your comfort zone, it gives this Lie room to grow. *It is normal to feel like a new version of yourself when you're playing a bigger game.*

The truth is that life only gives you what you're ready for. Got a new job? You are qualified for it, or you wouldn't have gotten it. Received an invitation to a women's leadership group filled with powerhouses? Congratulations, you must be a powerhouse too!

I remember my client, Kristy, whose Inner Mean Girl punished her with this Lie when she moved into her new home. It was twice the size of her former house and felt big and almost, gulp, dare she say it, showy. For the first few months she felt like the police were going to show up and arrest her for being an imposter. Once she understood her Inner Critic as the source of this Lie, she relaxed into her new home with gratitude for what she and her husband had created.

Challenge: The next time you feel the imposter Lie kicking in, take yourself through this process:

1. Ask yourself: What is the new growth opportunity at hand? (A new job? A big promotion? A book deal? A new possession?) In Kristy's case, it was moving into a bigger home.

2. How did you create this new opportunity or thing for yourself? Kristy and her husband worked their tails off to create the down payment for their new home. They also got lucky with some real estate deals and an inheritance, and created a vision board for their dream home. Hmm...after Kristy answered this question she finally got that they did create it after all!

3. What are the top three reasons you deserve it? Here are Kristy's: One, they needed more space, since their family was growing and both she and her husband work from home. Two, they honored her mother-in-law by caring for her, and spending part of the inheritance on their dream home is an homage to her. Three, it is her birthright to have a beautiful space to live in.

4. What does your Inner Wisdom know to be the Truth about this opportunity or thing? Kristy's Inner Wisdom knew that her home is a symbol of her and her husband's love, success, and joy. They give thanks for it nearly every day and appreciate and respect it.

As you unravel the imposter story, I know you'll discover the Truth about how much you deserve your new life! And your Inner Superstar will shine even brighter.

Affirmation: I joyfully accept the gifts in my life. I deserve all of them and know that life will never give me more than I can handle. (Hint: Feel free to insert your Inner Wisdom's Truth from question 4 above for your affirmation!)

"You are a living magnet."

— BRIAN TRACY, chairman and CEO of
Brian Tracy International, a company specializing in the
training and development of individuals and organizations

BIG FAT LIE #3

I am unlovable.

The Truth: Oh, sweetie, let's imagine that we're standing face-to-face. Let me have a moment with you — the real you. Please hear me out. We are *all* lovable. We are all worthy of being loved. *You* are lovable. No matter what you've done. No matter what mistakes you've made, there is a place of love just waiting for you. The first step in embracing this lovability is taking the stand to love yourself.

Cooper was a witty writer and a wonderful vegetarian cook, and she had an Inner Critic that was just brutal with this unlovable Lie. We named her Inner Mean Girl "Loveless Lulu." Loveless Lulu carried a martini in one hand and a cigarette in the other. She was always in the background, saying, "You are unlovable. Who will ever love you? You'll *never* be loved, kid."

After we named and drew Loveless Lulu, Cooper had a lightbulb moment. She realized that this Lie was her Inner Mean Girl's way of keeping her safe so that she would never be hurt or vulnerable. In other words, thinking she was safe from being wounded was the big payoff of believing she was unlovable. But the cost was way too high. With Loveless Lulu in charge, Cooper kept attracting men who treated her poorly, proving her "I'm unlovable" theory. Yet Cooper wanted to love, she wanted to receive true love, and she desperately wanted to stop the loveless self-talk. She began by starting a loving relationship with herself, and her life completely transformed. Not only did she become much happier in her own skin, but within one year she also ended up attracting her soulmate (they met at the farmers' market over some new spring radishes — I think it's so romantic that you never know when love will find you, don't you?) and is now happily married.

Challenge: Please find a quiet place to sit, and do the following visualization. (I'd love to lead you through this visualization. You can get it as a free download in your reader's tool kit at www .BigFatLiesTheBook.com.)

- Begin by taking ten deep breaths. Let the air fill your belly, then your lungs. Count each breath on the inhale, and notice how your breathing slows down and how lovely it is to just sit.
- Now imagine sitting across from yourself. You are looking into your own eyes.
- Look deeply into your eyes and simply notice...you.
- Notice how beautiful you are. Notice how kind you are. Notice what is working about you.
- Now notice the disappointments you carry with you. Notice the dreams that have yet to come true. Notice what isn't working.
- Imagine being your own best friend for a moment. What do you want to say to yourself, your dearest, most beloved friend?

- Really receive your own words.
- End your discussion with "I love you. You are so lovable."
- Notice the way your body feels as you say these words of love. Realize that this is the beginning of a beautiful friendship, a lifelong friendship that will stand the test of time.

Congratulations! You've just tapped into your Inner Superstar and Inner Wisdom, who love you unconditionally. They know how lovable you are.

Repeat this meditation daily for the next thirty to forty days. I guarantee you will shift your cellular programming and begin to see just how lovable you are.

Affirmation: Everyone is lovable, especially me.

"You, yourself, as much as anybody in the entire universe, deserve your love and affection."

— BUDDHA, spiritual teacher

I should have known better.

Can also show up as:

*I should have
done things differently.*

The Truth: If you had known better, you would have done better. We often act as if there is another version of us, the "perfect self," that is doing things substantially better than our "actual self." When we play the comparison game with this perfect self, we never measure up. The reality is that there is only the self that is present right here and now. Our actual self is doing the best she can. Let's take the word *should* out of our vocabulary and stop the perfect-self comparison game.

Sharon played this comparison game all the time. She was in the midst of writing her dissertation and constantly compared herself with her perfect self, feeling that she should be writing the dissertation in record time. Once we uncovered the game she was playing, we ended up laughing over it — big belly laughs. She was so relieved to stop playing the game of "beat the invisible clock." In the end, she finished her dissertation by her deadline and was very proud of her work.

Challenge: Become aware of when you play the perfect-self comparison game:

1. Begin by making a list of all the "shoulds" you've been putting on yourself.
2. Notice how these shoulds are holding you back.
3. Notice how good it feels to come clean with your should list.
4. Next forgive and acknowledge your real, present-day self.
5. Finally, change the word *should* on your list to the word *could*, and see how this lifts you into the land of possibility and inspiration. For example: "I should go to the gym three days a week" becomes "I could go to the gym three days a week"; "I should clean out the garage" becomes "I could clean out the garage"; "I should balance my checkbook" becomes "I could balance my checkbook."

Affirmation: I am always doing the best I can.

"There is good in everything."

— ERNEST HOLMES, American writer and spiritual teacher, founder of the Science of Mind

I don't measure up.

Can also show up as:

I am so much better than everyone else.

The Truth: It's kind of like gambling in Vegas. If you play the comparison game, you will eventually lose — every time. When you are on the "winning team" (i.e., you feel you're doing better, looking better, or achieving more), you lose by alienating yourself, coming off as arrogant, and creating distance instead of connection. When you're on the "losing team" (i.e., everyone else is looking better, doing better, and achieving far more than you are), you end up feeling horrible about yourself. And who wants that?

My dear friend Samantha Bennett, creator of the Organized Artist Company, once said to me, "It's like I'm in this gorgeous ballroom of my life and I'm focusing on the dust on the baseboards. And then I turn around and compare my baseboard's dust with someone else's ballroom. I'll never measure up that way." Yes! That's exactly right.

We will never know what's really going on in the lives of others.

We only know the truth of our own lives. So, step out of the comparison game and step into the gorgeous ballroom of your life!

Challenge: Give up the comparison game for good, and celebrate the ballroom of your life!

- Notice when you are most likely to play the comparison game. In other words, when do you look at the dust on your baseboards? Is it when you're thinking about money? Your weight or body image? Your love life? Your career?
- Decide to quit your comparison addiction cold turkey. My partner at Inner Mean Girl Reform School, Christine Arylo, loves calling this a "comparison diet." Just like a new eating plan has you turning away from unhealthy food, this comparison diet asks you to be strict with yourself about your unhealthy comparison thoughts.
- Gather a support team that will hold you accountable for staying "on the wagon." This team's job is to blow the whistle whenever you play the comparison game and to encourage you to focus on what you have — your gorgeous ballroom. Call your team members whenever you feel yourself heading down the comparison path.
- Express gratitude for all that the ballroom of your life has to offer. Remember: many people have successfully given up addictions by going cold turkey. Let this inspire you to stop playing the comparison game.

Affirmation: I lift my eyes above the baseboards to see the whole picture of my life, full and glorious and incomparable!

> *"The rose does best as a rose. Lilies make the best lilies. And look! You — the best you around!"*
> — RUMI, thirteenth-century Persian poet and Sufi mystic

*If it weren't for me,
nothing would get done.*

Can also show up as:

*I sacrifice and sacrifice,
and no one cares.*

The Truth: If this Lie sounds familiar, then I hate to break it to you: you're acting like a martyr. Taking on the role of a martyr is a choice. I'm ready to live up to my name — the Wake-Up Call Coach — so get ready. If you feel like you are constantly sacrificing, only *you* hold the power to knock it off! And I say that as a loving truth, my dear. When you're in martyr mode, that means one of two things:

1. You want attention and something to complain about, in which case it's time to come clean with your need for negative attention. You are colluding with misery. Your double-dog dare is to go complaint free for thirty days and to discover what a creative problem solver you are.

2. Or you truly have a desire to be in service and contribute but are doing so at a cost to yourself, in which case you must take a step back and take care of yourself first. Your

double-dog dare is to make yourself your top priority before you help those around you. Really. It's time.

Challenge: Imagine that your life is a big closet filled with different outfits that represent different attitudes. Inside there is the outfit of power, the outfit of joy, the outfit of victimization, and so on. Slip on the martyr outfit and see what it feels like. What does it look like? How does it fit? Is it in your comfort zone — a dress you frequently wear? Is it unfamiliar? Really be honest here. What are the costs of wearing the martyr outfit all the time? Are there any payoffs? Decide to keep this outfit in your closet but not to wear it all the time. Or maybe you want to haul it to Goodwill right now! What other outfits might you try on for size?

Affirmation: I am *empowered,* and I choose to take care of me first!

"I am the master of my fate. I am the captain of my soul."
— from "Invictus," by WILLIAM ERNEST HENLEY,
English poet, critic, and editor

I'm so ashamed.

The Truth: There are two types of shame. There's the shame that comes from mistakes you have made. Then there's the shame that comes from things that have happened to you, events that were beyond your control. However, the common thread is that when you feel shame, you are focusing on your past — your past mistakes or shameful things you have endured.

If you feel ashamed of your actions and ways of being, it's time to name your mistakes, no matter how awful, and claim them as an opportunity for growth and learning. The bottom line is that shame does not serve you well; it suffocates hope, new lessons, and growth. Decide to forgive yourself.

If your source of shame is things that have occurred that were beyond your control, take heart in the story of Greg, a musician and a longtime client of mine, who was ashamed of the abuse he had endured as a child. Rationally, he knew his shame was unwarranted. He was a child when the abuse happened, after all, and his sense of responsibility was misplaced. He had also done years of therapy with a wonderful therapist about this trauma and really processed it. (I trust that you will never go deeper into a shameful memory than is safe for you, and I also trust that you will seek help from a support group or a therapeutic professional if you need to. Don't let pride or fear get in the way of you getting all the help you need, okay?) As Greg and I drilled down, we uncovered that he felt ashamed of not standing up for himself, even though he was very young when the abuse occurred. He felt ashamed of not telling an adult who could have helped him, despite the threats from his perpetrator. It was a ridiculous notion that his Inner Critic beat him up with. Somehow he thought a child could overpower an adult — talk about a Big Fat Lie. I helped Greg start to let go of his shame by suggesting that he speak kindly and gently to himself, as he would to a best friend or child. He began to see himself in a new light and with new compassion, and at last he released his false sense of responsibility for the abuse. It was like the scene in the film *Good Will Hunting*, in which Robin Williams's character (the therapist) says to Matt Damon's character (the patient) over and over, "It's not your fault" until Matt Damon breaks down in tears, releasing once and for all the shame of what he had endured as a child.

Your power lies in the present, so let's work on releasing your shame right now.

Challenge: Start by asking yourself the following questions:

1. What am I ashamed of? Get specific and real. Notice if you feel shame about how you've acted or who you've been, or if you are feeling shame because you are taking responsibility for another's shameful acts. If it's the latter, please continue to peel back the layers as Greg did, and see if you are feeling shame for not standing up for

yourself or speaking out, no matter how unrealistic those expectations may be.

2. What is your Inner Critic saying to you about this situation? Bring the words that are tormenting and shaming you out of the darkness and into the light.

3. Close your eyes, take a deep breath, and ask, "What does my Inner Wisdom know?"

4. Write down your Inner Wisdom's Truth, and say it aloud to yourself while making your Inner Wisdom's physical gesture, as described in the introduction.

5. Ask yourself, "How would I respond to a dear friend if he or she were feeling this shame?" Find compassionate words.

6. Now, take your response from the question above and speak to yourself the way you would to a friend. Perhaps you say compassionately, "Hey, everyone makes mistakes. It sounds like you are becoming clearer about what you want from your life — that's a good thing!" or "You are a good person *and* you screwed up. What did you learn?" or "I'm ready to release the responsibility I feel for the shameful acts of others. I am ready to heal."

7. Finally, do a release ritual. Fill in the blanks in the following sentences, and then say the sentences aloud. It can help to stand tall, and even to put your arms out, to feel a sense of surrender. Maybe you even want to light a candle or go to a place you love (a beach, church, or favorite hiking trail). It can be especially powerful to be witnessed in this ritual by a loved one. Ask her to respond, "So be it."

    A. You say, "I hereby release all shame I have about
    _____ [say the name of the experience only — do not go into the story of the details]. I surrender it for healing to the universe/God/

source energy. I am ready to claim the lessons from this experience, and I now trust that this experience was in my highest good. I forgive myself and _____ [list any others you might need to forgive, if appropriate]. I know that _____ [fill in the blank with your words from step 6]. All is well. So be it."

Affirmation: Take your responses to steps 5 and 6 and repeat them daily for thirty days.

"To understand is to forgive, even oneself."

— ALEXANDER CHASE, American journalist

BIG FAT LIE #8

I am damaged goods.

The Truth: First of all, ouch! My eyes always tear up when I hear people utter this Lie. It brings to mind the reject pile at the clothing store that goes on sale for half off because of the slightest rip or tear. And *you*, my sweet one, are *not* damaged goods, and you most certainly don't belong in the reject pile. Deep inside your Inner Superstar is just waiting for the opportunity to shine.

Here's what I know to be true: You can leave behind any piece of your past that you choose, at any time. You have the power to uncover the gifts your pain has brought you and to ditch the rest. At any moment, you can create a fresh start. And when you do, you'll find that you will attract an entirely new experience. New people, new circumstances, a new life. One that is worthy of you.

Challenge: If you have fallen prey to the damaged goods Lie, it's time to redefine your relationship with yourself. What past events have led you to believe that you're damaged goods? (The exercise below is designed to help you dissolve the power of this Lie by understanding its source. If a memory surfaces that feels too charged, please make sure to reach out to a mental health professional to get the support you deserve.) Follow the process below:

- Start by closing your eyes and thinking the Lie "I am damaged goods," and notice where you feel it in your body. Do you feel a lump in your throat? Heat in your hands?
- Next, breathe into that area of your body and notice how old you feel and what memories surface. Are you sixteen being teased by a boy you like?
- How much power did you have over those events? For example, if being berated by your third-grade gym teacher is stuck in your body, how much could you have prevented that adult from humiliating you? (Guess what — no child can defend herself against an adult, particularly an authoritative adult who is supposed to be taking care of her.)
- How much power do you have *now* over how you think about those events? Hint: This is where all your power lies — in how you now choose to frame these events for yourself.
- What three experiences can you call to mind to help you feel powerful now? When you go on a run? When you stand tall and confident at work as you present your ideas to your team? When you gave birth to your baby?
- If you were speaking to your past self about troubling events, what would you say to her? Write a letter to your past self (maybe your eight-year-old self or your twenty-year-old self) expressing how you feel.

- Now, make the commitment to get to know your present-day, powerful self by setting up a weekly or monthly date night with yourself. Yes, you are now dating fabulous you! Perhaps you take yourself out to the movies on this special date night, write in your journal at a coffee shop, or take a hot bath. The idea is for you to get to know *you* in the present moment.

Affirmation: I am whole. I am loved. I am powerful.

"Everybody is damaged goods.
Everybody got bumps and dents, ja?"
— PAUL QUARRINGTON, Canadian playwright,
novelist, and filmmaker

I don't belong.

Can also show up as:

*I don't fit in. I'm different.
I'm special.*

The Truth: This Lie is really common. And really painful. It's hard to feel like your nose is pressed up against the glass, like you're always an outsider watching the party and never getting to participate.

But this Lie is also really slippery! There is a big payoff for this Lie, so there is a fine edge to walk here. After all, I want you to feel special and unique and to celebrate being the one and only ever *you*. But I don't want you to slip into the land of being isolated because of your differences, keeping yourself away from the world. I want you to feel embraced, loved, and supported by your tribe!

Rachel had an Inner Mean Girl who loved to beat her up by telling her that she didn't belong. It began in middle school when she felt like the clique of popular girls was off having a great time, while she felt insecure and alone. The truth, of course, is that even the girls who were popular were riddled with insecurity, self-doubt, and the intense desire to fit in. We all have pain in puberty, honey!

As an adult Rachel realized that she wasn't even trying to belong anymore. It was less painful to believe that she just didn't belong than it was to reach out, to risk, and to create connection. This is how sneaky this Lie can be. Believing you don't fit in can serve as self-protection. It keeps you safe but often unhappy and downright lonely. It's time to step out of this Lie!

Challenge: As your coach, I'm really curious about the edge of this Lie for you. Answer the questions below to investigate:

- How are you celebrating your uniqueness?
- What is the connection between seeing yourself as different or special and feeling as if you don't belong?
- How are you isolating yourself? How do *you* contribute to your sense of not belonging? Really take responsibility for the ways you withdraw, hide, or pull away.
- Where is the line for you between celebrating your fabulousness and uniqueness and feeling isolated, different, and alone?
- How *do* you fit in? Which people support you? What tribe have you created where you can be 100 percent you?
- For forty-eight hours, I want you to collect evidence of how much you belong. Take note of when you feel yourself fitting in. Notice the invitations, welcoming smiles, and offers you receive.
- If you don't feel that you have a tribe, your double-dog dare is to begin to create one. You are a leader, after all. So go lead and create your community. It is waiting for you!

Affirmation: I belong to me. I am invited. I celebrate me.

> *"Those who matter don't mind
> and those who mind don't matter."*
> — BERNARD BARUCH, American financier and statesman

BIG FAT LIE #10

I am powerless.

Can also show up as:

The world is against me.

The Truth: We are very powerful — so powerful that we can actually choose to *disempower ourselves.* And sometimes it is downright easier to be a victim. When you're a victim, you don't have to take any responsibility for what is happening to you. Instead, you get to sit back and be miserable (and, as we all know, misery loves company!). However, there are immense downsides to being a victim: it's boring and depressing, and it makes you feel like your life is pointless.

On the other hand, using your power to take responsibility can be a whole lot of fun. The act of being in command may be a little frightening at first, but it allows you to become the master of your universe. It allows for a true sense of freedom. It allows for adventure and creativity.

Challenge: Step out of the victim mentality by noticing what you do have power over. Answer the following questions:

- How much power do you have over your emotional state? Look closely here. We can sometimes feel victimized by our emotions. But emotions stem from thoughts, and thoughts are manageable when you're mindful. This is why I encourage affirmations and tuning in to your Inner Wisdom's Truth (and ditching your Inner Critic's Big Fat Lies). A more flexible mind-set will allow you to start planting the seeds for positive thoughts — and when you are thinking good thoughts, you feel good!

- How often do you say no to whomever or whatever is victimizing you? As adults, we have a choice in almost every situation... *if* we look for it. You can quit your job. You can end a friendship that doesn't work. You can even renegotiate your agreements with yourself so you feel more empowered!

- Is being a victim a knee-jerk response when you feel vulnerable? Yikes! Here's a comfort zone that not only is uncomfortable, it's excruciating. I just loathe these patterns we create that habitually lead us to feel bad. Notice the patterns of your own victim responses.

- When and where in your life do you feel powerful? Notice what sensations feeling powerful creates in your body. Do you feel taller? Walk differently? Explore powerful postures, and bring them with you when you know you are going to be around people or in situations that can make you feel victimized. For example, go to your work meeting dressed in a power suit, take a prominent chair, and sit tall and decide to feel powerful. Notice your results!

- For one week try on a new perspective that will make you feel more powerful, such as the "I can do it" perspective; the "superwoman" perspective; the "ready to rumble" perspective; or the "not taking my life too seriously" perspective.

- Live your chosen perspective for a week. See what happens!

Affirmation: Write a new affirmation for yourself based on the perspective you created for yourself. Maybe it's "I am a victor!" or "I am (super)woman, hear me roar!" — whatever feels exciting and energizing!

> *"I've always been the opposite of a paranoid.*
> *I operate as if everyone is part of a plot to enhance*
> *my well-being."*

— STAN DALE, founder of the Human Awareness Institute and national radio personality

BIG FAT LIE #11

It's too late for me.

The Truth: There is no time like the present. The form this Lie takes really doesn't matter. Maybe your Inner Critic harps on you about your career, saying, "It's too late for me to change careers," or your love life, saying, "It's too late for me to find love," or learning new things, saying, "It's too late to teach this old dog new tricks." The bottom line is that since you are alive and reading this book, you still have time to go for it!

A truly inspiring example of the *it's never too late* mind-set is the story of George Dawson, as featured on *The Oprah Winfrey Show*. At the age of ninety-eight, George decided to finally end the legacy of illiteracy in his family and learn to read. On his hundredth birthday, Mr. Dawson was able to read his birthday cards for the first time in his life. How's that for proof?

Challenge: See what this Lie is really about by following the steps below:

- First, get really clear on where you are using the too late Lie as an excuse. Do you believe it is too late to get your college degree? Too late to learn how to paint? Too late to get in shape?
- Notice what this Lie is robbing you of. The possibility of love? A new career path? A chance to strut your stuff on the beach? Drink in the dream you've been denying yourself. What is it you really, really want?
- What is the worst thing that could happen if you just go for it? Allow your Inner Critic to run the worst-case scenario. Does she believe you'll end up heartbroken? That you'll fail your exams and flunk out? That your movie script won't get sold?
- Notice how your Inner Mean Girl is protecting you. She thinks that if you don't try, then you won't be hurt. Her mantra is "I can save myself from failure and pain if I don't go for it." The truth is that you're in pain anyway when you beat yourself up with this excuse. The desire for your dream is there, whether or not you acknowledge it, causing you torment.
- Now run the best-case scenario. What is the best thing that could happen if you go for it? What is the most sublime dream possible? You get the degree and feel like a million bucks? You find the love of your life and live happily ever after? You sell a painting and know it is being treasured by another?
- Look for evidence of those who've gone for it, even if it seemed "too late" for them. You'll find inspiring stories like George Dawson's! My client Jennifer uncovered the story of a woman who learned to paint at the age of eighty-three. Take heart in the woman who met the love of her life at age sixty-seven, as my friend Judy's mom did.

- Check in with yourself, and notice that you can handle both the worst- and the best-case scenario. Take a risk, feel the fear, and go for it!

Affirmation: I am ready to blossom now.

> *"And the day came when the risk to remain tight*
> *in a bud was more painful*
> *than the risk it took to blossom."*
>
> — ANAÏS NIN, French-Cuban writer

When I get _____,
then I'll be happy.

Can also show up as:

When I am _____,
then I'll be happy.

The Truth: This Lie is extremely prevalent in modern society. Our happiness can actually be separate from our circumstances — in fact, we *must* learn to separate our happiness from our circumstances. Otherwise, we are continuously chasing a carrot tied to a stick, dangling just out of reach. As soon as you reach your goal and have that new car or new house, get that promotion, or lose the weight, you'll be on to your next desire, your next happiness carrot.

Look back on things you have obtained. You thought each one would be the cure-all, but it wasn't, was it? Being in a state of desire is part of the human experience. Once we attain the object of one desire, we are on to the quest for the next one. A prime example of the when/then myth is a study conducted by PNC Advisers, a Pittsburgh-based firm that advises the wealthy. More than a third of the millionaires surveyed said that having enough money was a constant worry and that they'd feel more secure if only they had twice as much. The person with $2 million is sure he'd feel secure with $4 million, the fellow with $4 million claims that $8 million would bring him security and happiness, the woman with a billion would finally feel satisfied with $2 billion...when does it end? It doesn't. With that in mind, let's claim our joy and happiness *now*. Let's enjoy every step of the journey, leaping from desire to desire, without attachments or illusions.

Challenge: Make a list of what you appreciate about your life. Next, make a list of all your desires: short-term, long-term, tangible ("weigh 155 pounds"), and intangible ("I want to feel vibrant and healthy"). Choose one appreciation and one desire to focus on each day. Expressing gratitude for your life today as well as your desires for what you want next will allow you to experience the delicious anticipation of what's to come.

Marge took on this challenge and discovered that she had been allowing her sense of deficiency to get in the way of achieving her goals. This is a common occurrence. Whenever Marge allowed herself to want something, she would immediately feel that she was "not there yet," leaving her deflated and depressed. Her misguided solution was to reduce her desire so that she would feel better, which just led to an uninspired, mediocre existence. After completing this challenge, she began *anticipating* the things she desired, while feeling appreciation and gratitude for what she did have. She allowed desire to come back into her life and started having fun again. She also began to get more of what she wanted!

Affirmation: I am happy, content, *and* eager for more delicious things!

> *"There are two things to aim at in life:*
> *first to get what you want, and after that to enjoy it.*
> *Only the wisest of mankind has achieved the second."*
> — LOGAN PEARSALL SMITH, American essayist and critic

Self-criticism is effective.

Can also show up as:

The way to accomplish things is by being hard on myself.

The Truth: Finding a way to nourish yourself with unconditional self-love and self-compassion is not only the most feel-good, wonderful gift you can give yourself, but it is also the most effective way for you to create more of what you want in your life. Think of it like parenting. When a child is learning to walk, we don't belittle, criticize, or berate her every time she falls down. Instead, we encourage, cheerlead, and normalize the process of failing as part of the human experience. Study after study has shown that this kind of parenting is far more effective than spanking, fear mongering, or belittling.

The same is true in our relationship with ourselves. The more we practice inward loving-kindness, the more happiness and joy we experience. And with that foundation of unconditional love and support in place, we experience more success. I've seen people fall into the trap of thinking that if they go too easy on themselves and lighten up, they will fall into self-indulgence and spiral out of control. Believe me when I tell you that after more than a decade of coaching, I have not once found that to be true. Instead, I see self-love and self-compassion as the ticket to a new lease on life and more everyday bliss. After all, life is too short to miss out on even one drop of joy!

Challenge: Start being kinder to yourself now by following the process below:

- First, bring your attention to how you are being hard on yourself. Whenever I ask a woman, "Where are you being hard on yourself?" she usually tears up, because she knows exactly how she is beating herself up. It can feel a bit embarrassing or even shameful to admit how hard we are on ourselves.

- Ponder what you fear will happen if you lighten up. For example, if you are berating yourself about how much you weigh, you might be fearful that if you stop being hard on yourself about your weight you will spiral into a fit of binge eating. If you are beating yourself up about not having a romantic partner, you may fear that if you let go and lighten up, you'll stop dating altogether and end up alone forever. Isn't it remarkable to notice how our Inner Critics just love to speak in absolutes? Our Inner Critics just love to use the words *always* and *forever* and *never*. Often you can transform your frame of mind just by substituting absolutes with *sometimes* or *just for today*. Magical, isn't it?

- Notice what the beating-yourself-up cycle actually does. There's some real irony here. I've found that being hard on ourselves often causes the thing we're most afraid of. In other words, it's when we are beating ourselves up that we end up binge eating or picking Mr. Wrong…again.

- Make a decision to experiment with self-compassion and self-love. What would a radical act of loving-kindness toward yourself look like in this area of your life? Would it mean taking yourself off of Match.com and spending time with your girlfriends instead? How about loving yourself enough to spend time each week at a local farmers' market buying fresh vegetables and fruits that you adore?
- Lighten up. Really gain some perspective about this area of your life. See the big picture of what a badass you are in other areas of your life. Nourish and celebrate your magnificence.

Affirmation: Loving myself is the most important thing I do... and I'm lightening up more and more each day.

> *"Self-compassion is really conducive to motivation.... With self-compassion, if you care about yourself, you do what's healthy for you rather than what's harmful to you."*
>
> — DR. KRISTIN NEFF,
> author and professor of human development and culture

BIG FAT LIES
ABOUT BODY AND SELF-CARE

My daughter, Annabella, is three years old as I type this. Her photograph sits on my desk, capturing her in all her mischief and glory. Annabella recently began taking a ballet class, and I marvel at the way she looks at herself in the mirror as she dances. She gazes lovingly at herself in her tutu, filled with curiosity. She has absolutely no judgment of or self-consciousness about herself or the way she looks. Just pure love and inquisitiveness. She is filled with wonder as she turns and dances about. I stare lovingly at her, beaming with pride and inspiration. When my guard is down, my Inner Mean Girl steps in with these types of questions: "When will self-love stop and self-criticism seep in? At what point should I expect my daughter to look into the mirror with self-loathing? When will she stop the wonder and curiosity and begin to see a litany of things she wants to change about how she looks?" Gulp.

I crave a day when we, as grown-ups, can look in the mirror with the love, kindness, and respect of a three-year-old. When we step out of harsh judgments and into compassion. It's a tall order, isn't it? Here's the thing: we have a lot to break through. The advertising industry has made billions of dollars from selling us the idea that we're not enough. Not young enough. Not beautiful enough. Not thin enough. Too flat chested. Too big in the hips. Name the thing you dislike the most when you look in the mirror, and you'll find a plethora of external "solutions" for it everywhere you look.

Our subconscious minds are eating up all these negative images every single day. Studies show that only 8 percent of the images we consume are registered by our conscious mind. That means that 92 percent of the airbrushed, stick-thin, perfectly proportioned images infiltrate our subconscious minds, influencing the way we feel about ourselves. It's an onslaught of insanity: all these unattainable bodies put before us as an ideal to strive for. As the supermodel Cindy Crawford once said when looking at her airbrushed, Photoshopped pictures, "*I* don't even look like Cindy Crawford."

We need to consciously work to win back our thoughts about how we are supposed to look. We need to overcome the Big Fat Lies about our bodies and our self-care. We need to tune in to our Inner Wisdom on a deep level and to practice, practice, practice, so that we can model a healthy relationship with ourselves. If not for your own happiness, then do it for the Annabellas of the world. Our little girls need us to become beacons of self-love. Let's begin *now*.

BIG FAT LIE #14

I'm too _____
[fat, thin, ugly, tall].

The Truth: I don't know a single woman who doesn't want to change her looks in some way. How could we *not* feel this way, when practically since birth our subconscious minds have been bombarded by images of flawless womenlike creatures? According to media expert Jean Kilbourne, the average American is exposed to three thousand ads every day! And almost every one of those ads is telling us that we are not enough and is selling us something to make us look better, younger, thinner. Really allow that to sink in for a minute.

So when you look in the mirror and find your Inner Critic flagellating you with words such as *fat, ugly,* or *too old,* take a moment to ask yourself: Too fat compared to whom? Too old compared to what image? Too ugly compared to what supermodel (who's been airbrushed and Photoshopped to death)?

Notice what this belief is holding you back from. Are you really saying that you think you're too fat to be loved? To attract a great business partner? Or that you're too old to go for your dream job? Or learn how to sculpt? Find the love of your life? These assumptions can stop us in our tracks.

Challenge: Because this Lie is so pervasive, I'm going to give you an extra dose of coaching love by giving you several powerful questions and tools below. Get crackin', beautiful!

- What are you hardest on yourself about when it comes to your looks?
- What does your Inner Mean Girl believe this "flaw" is keeping you from? A relationship? A promotion?
- How true is that assumption? In other words, is your weight really keeping you from finding a mate? Is your big nose preventing that career change? What you'll notice is that 99 percent of the time *you* are keeping you from what you want, not the wrinkles around your eyes or the size of your hips!
- Now imagine for a minute that this physical characteristic is not stopping you from getting what you want. Really breathe that in.
- Think of a person who is also too fat, too old, or too whatever-you-think-you-are who does have the success, love, or career that you want. For example, let's say you believe you're too ugly to find love. Think about a famous person known for his or her "character face" who is crazy in love with a soulmate! Think about your dear friend who has been with her high school sweetheart since they were both pimply faced and awkward.
- Finally, look at the whole person that you are by filling in the blanks: I am too [insert the negative characteristic] and I'm also [insert things you love that are also true

about you]. For example, "I'm too old...and I'm also very energetic, a great baker, and a movie buff." "I'm too flat chested...and I'm also loving, funny, a team player, and great in the sack!" "I'm too ugly...and I'm also a wonderful mother and a great friend, and I love to hike."

Affirmation: I am beautiful, sexy, and strong just the way I am.

"To wish you were someone else
is to waste the person you are."
— UNKNOWN

Taking care of myself is selfish.

The Truth: When we put our own well-being first, we are more able to be there for others. I know how hard it can be to carve out personal time...boy, do I know! But it is *vital* to do so to be a present and caring woman. By deciding to take responsibility for your self-care, you are giving yourself the opportunity to be a good parent, friend, partner, sibling, and/or coworker. As the author and incredibly inspiring speaker Lisa Nichols stated during the Women Masters tele-seminar interview I did with her, you must stop giving from a full cup. Instead, make your cup over-flow so much so that you give only from the *saucer*. (If you have yet to do so, make sure to register for your reader's tool kit, where you'll receive Lisa's inspiring Women Masters interview! Go to www.BigFatLiesTheBook.com.)

As a working mom, I can speak firsthand about the need for self-care and the struggle it can be to find the time for it. I know from experience how vital it is to take time to recharge so that you can be the best mother possible. During the first few months of my daughter's life, it was incredibly tough to find any time for myself. I have a supportive husband and a wonderful family nearby, but I chose to breastfeed and therefore was the one responsible for feeding the baby every few hours or so. After a month, I was so worn out that I would cry at the drop of a hat. I realized I needed to walk my talk and take twenty to thirty minutes out for *me time* each day, whether that meant taking a bath, going on a gratitude walk, or meditating. It amazed me how selfish I felt by taking time for myself, but it also amazed me how much more I had to offer after I had rejuvenated.

Challenge: Announce to those you love that you are making self-care a top priority. Make a list of the things that you know rejuvenate and refuel you (taking walks in nature, taking long baths, working out, journaling, playing piano, doing yoga, scrapbooking, quilting, having coffee with friends, mediating, doing a crossword puzzle — whatever works for you). Then, carve out and schedule self-care time each week — a minimum of one hour a week that you hold just as sacred as the other appointments in your calendar. Work your way up to daily self-care time. Here are some other examples of me time:

- singing along to your favorite tunes on your iPod during an hour of exercise
- baking
- reading a great book
- sightseeing (going to museums, theater, parks, the beach)

Affirmation: I give myself permission to take care of me first. My cup runneth over!

"Love yourself first and the rest of your life will fall into place."
— LUCILLE BALL, American comedian and actress

One of these days
I'll win the battle of the bulge.

The Truth: Sugar, take it from me, there is no winning because there is no battle. There is only you and your relationship with your body — your miraculous body. Your body finds a way to breathe, move, dance, laugh, sigh, gulp, run, and crawl. It's high time you started appreciating it. Give up the battle, and start celebrating your body *today*.

When we allow the battle of the bulge Lie to fester, we contribute to a feeling of literally being in a battle. Really think about this expression for a moment: being in a battle means there is violence, hatred, and war. Let's decide to delete this expression from our repertoire, shall we? Plus, as we buy into this battle myth, we also end up resisting the release of those extra pounds (assuming that is the goal). Do you think a war zone is an easy place to plant the seeds of health, vibrancy, and sexiness? Me neither! Instead we must create acceptance of and peace with our bodies as they are right now, in this moment, and from that accepting, compassionate, loving mind-set, we can find well-being and joie de vivre.

Challenge: Okay, are you ready? Are you willing? Do you dare? Let's go for radical self-acceptance here:

- Stand *naked* in front of the mirror and name ten things you love about yourself every day for a week. Yes, that's right: ten things you love. They can range from "great ass" to "the miracle of my skin" to "my heart is pumping."
- Express your gratitude for your miraculous body by being vigilant about the way you talk about it to others and yourself — stop the cruelty, the complaints, and the self-effacing humor. For example, when someone compliments you, instead of deflecting with, "Really? Gosh, I just can't stand my thighs in this," say, "Thank you so much. I'm feeling pretty sassy today!" or "Thanks for noticing...I've been walking a lot and feel great." When you get ready each morning, instead of complaining to yourself about how your jeans fit, move on to the dress that is flirty and fun and that makes you feel like a million bucks.

Affirmation: My body is a miracle, and it reflects my divine self.

> *"My limbs are made glorious*
> *by the touch of this world of life."*
>
> — RABINDRANATH TAGORE,
> Bengali poet, playwright, and painter

I cannot ask for help or support
unless I'm in crisis.

Can also show up as:

Asking for help is weak.

The Truth: I see this Lie especially among caretakers and moms. We have this expectation that we should be able to take care of everything ourselves, all the time. In reality, we deserve support and help all the time. It really does take a village, people!

It is okay to ask for help when you're doing well. In fact, asking for support as part of *preventive* care is vital. When you commit to asking for support consistently, you are *inspiring* others to do the same for themselves. You can be a shining example. Shine, baby, shine!

Challenge: Pinpoint the areas in your life where you could use some help, and decide who will make up your support team. Ask these people if they are willing to be on your team. Let them know they have a right to say no whenever they'd like. This agreement is vital, since you want them giving from their saucer too. Now make your first request.

If you are resistant to this exercise, maybe you find some satisfaction in waiting for a crisis before asking for assistance. Ask yourself: What is the payoff? Do I enjoy the rush of being in crisis? Is there some satisfaction to be had in getting more attention? Do I like being a martyr or a victim? If yes to martyr, see Big Fat Lie #6: "If it weren't for me, nothing would get done." If victim, see Big Fat Lie #10: "I am powerless."

Affirmation: I love to help, and I love to accept help!

> *"Turn the kindness spotlight inward."*
> — SARK, American author and artist

If I say no, people won't like me.

Can also show up as:

If I say no, I will be punished.
If I say no, I'm a bad girl.

The Truth: When you say no, you teach people how to honor and respect you. You also establish boundaries that allow people to understand what works and what doesn't work for you. You may find that some people cannot handle these boundaries. If so, it's time to reconsider those relationships and either move on and release the relationship altogether or create a relationship with those people that allows you to feel respected.

If you say yes when you're thinking no, you aren't letting people see the real you. This creates distance between you and your loved ones and will make you feel unhappy and disrespected.

Challenge: Throw out your Nice Girl hat and put on your 100 Percent Me hat instead. Start telling people how you really feel, start setting boundaries, and start saying no! Begin this process when you are with those closest to you. Let them know that you are practicing being authentic and dropping the "yes" act, and ask them to respect your boundaries. Try the following script to get started:

> You: Hi, _____ [fill in your trusted loved one's name]. Have you noticed that I have a bad habit of saying yes when I really want or need to say *no*?
>
> Loved one: As a matter of fact, I have noticed that.
>
> You: Well, I've decided that I am going to start setting some boundaries by saying no. I've realized that by saying yes all the time, I'm not expressing the way I really feel. I end up doing things that I don't want to do and, as a result, I'm becoming resentful. In essence, I'm hiding behind my yeses.
>
> Loved one: I didn't know that. Thank you for telling me. I really get it.
>
> You: I could really use your support here. Will you be there for me as I practice saying no, drawing boundaries, and being more authentic?
>
> Loved one: Absolutely! I am really proud of you and am delighted to help. You are an inspiration.

Those who love you will be thrilled that you trust them enough to let them in and will respect you even more for taking such initiative. When you start saying no, you will experience increased self-respect and self-adoration. I promise.

Affirmation: I say no when I want to, and people love me just the same.

> *"The most exhausting thing in life is being insincere."*
> — ANNE MORROW LINDBERGH, American author and aviator

BIG FAT LIE #19

*I have no control
over my body and my health.*

The Truth: According to a recent study done by the National Institutes of Health, 70 percent of all disease is stress related. The World Health Organization also warns of an increasing incidence of stress-related depression. So it seems we have immense power over our health. I've said it over and over: self-care must become your number one priority, and your health is one of the most important aspects of self-care.

Here's what the American Institute of Stress has to say:

The term "stress," as it is currently used, was coined by Hans Selye in 1936, who defined it as "the non-specific response of the body to any demand for change." Selye had noted in numerous experiments that laboratory animals subjected to acute but different noxious physical and emotional stimuli (blaring light, deafening noise, extremes of heat or cold, perpetual frustration) all exhibited the same pathologic changes of stomach ulcerations, shrinkage of lymphoid tissue, and enlargement of the adrenals. He later demonstrated that persistent stress could cause these animals to develop various diseases similar to those seen in humans, such as heart attacks, stroke, kidney disease, and rheumatoid arthritis.

So if stress is what happens when we do not respond to the demand for change, and we live in an ever-changing world, we need to find a way to cope, stay calm despite circumstances, and become mindful about our self-care. We gotta find some inner peace, honey!

Challenge: Take a health inventory of your life. The goal is to agree with all the statements below. If you don't, listen to your body's request to make a change, and commit to implementing a lifestyle change today.

- ✔ I exercise at least thirty minutes three days a week.
- ✔ I do not smoke.
- ✔ I use alcohol in moderation or not at all.
- ✔ I use antibiotics sparingly, and only in the case of a bacterial infection, never for a virus.
- ✔ I take a daily multivitamin.
- ✔ I drink plenty of water each day.
- ✔ I eat plenty of fruits and vegetables daily.
- ✔ I am at a healthy body weight.
- ✔ I get fresh air every day.
- ✔ I wear sunscreen daily.
- ✔ I enjoy at least one belly laugh each day.
- ✔ I get at least two hugs a day.
- ✔ I spend at least ten minutes each day focusing on positive things (e.g., my desires, goals, intentions) perhaps by meditating, visualizing, or breathing deeply.

✔ I connect with my Inner Wisdom and Inner Superstar daily, especially before I make big decisions.

As you work your way through this book and start tuning out the voice of your Inner Critic, I think you will notice that your health is improving....

Affirmation: I am healthy because I respond well to change. I am both adaptable and strong.

"The body manifests what the mind harbors."

— JERRY AUGUSTINE, American professional baseball player

*I am entitled
to have others take care of me.*

The Truth: From the recession and blowups on Wall Street to disaster relief efforts to Social Security to health care, the message is loud and clear: stop putting your well-being in the hands of others! Sure, our politicians and CEOs love to tell us they can ensure our safety, financial future, and health, but they can't. I'll even give them the benefit of the doubt by saying that most of them have good intentions (I don't want to be too cynical), but the fact remains that government and big business are simply not capable of fulfilling everyone's needs. The only person who you can know for sure will make your well-being a top priority is you, so please — take your power back.

Challenge: Make a list of all the ways you are relying on others to take care of you. Are you investing in your company's 401(k) and leaving it up to them to decide where your money goes? Are you hoping that Social Security will cover your retirement needs? Are you going without health coverage? Are you trusting large restaurant chains to attend to your nutrition? Next, decide to take charge of your care in one area each month. Learn how you can take your power back in a big way!

Affirmation: I am empowered. I take care of myself and my family with ease and grace.

"Men are made stronger on the realization that the helping hand they need is at the end of their own arm."

— SIDNEY J. PHILLIPS, World War II veteran

BIG FAT LIES ABOUT SUCCESS

*O*ne *of the most important things* you can do is to define what success means to you. So take a moment now and answer these questions:

- What does success mean to you?
- What is your unique vision of success?
- How will you know when you've achieved success?
- Imagine for a moment that you feel 100 percent successful. What would your life look like? Would you be traveling the world? Working with women in Darfur? Spending time with your family? Baking all day? Really get a sense of what a successful life looks like to you.

What most of my clients discover is that success has little to do with money or celebrity and much more to do with happiness and fulfillment. Our Inner Critics love to keep us running fast on the hamster wheel of alleged success, working harder and harder, getting nowhere, and missing the joy of simply being alive. I want you to have a deep sense of meaning and purpose in your life, to really take stock of what true happiness and success mean to you. This parable brilliantly illustrates the point.

The Fisherman and the Investment Banker

An American investment banker was on a pier in a small coastal Mexican village, when a small boat with just one fisherman docked. Inside the small boat were several large yellowfin tuna. The American complimented the Mexican on the quality of his fish and asked how long it had taken to catch them.

The fisherman replied, "Only a little while."

The American then asked why he didn't stay out longer and catch more fish.

The fisherman said he had enough to support his family's immediate needs.

The American then asked, "But what do you do with the rest of your time?"

The fisherman said, "I sleep late, fish a little, play with my children, take a siesta with my wife, Maria, and each evening I stroll into the village, where I sip wine and play guitar with my amigos. I have a full and busy life."

The American scoffed, "I am a Harvard MBA and could help you. You should spend more time fishing and with the proceeds, buy a bigger boat. With the proceeds from the bigger boat you could buy several boats...eventually you would have a fleet of fishing boats. Instead of selling your catch to a middleman you would sell directly to the processor, eventually opening your own cannery. You would control the product, processing, and distribution. You would need to leave this small coastal fishing village and move to Mexico City, then Los Angeles, and eventually New York City, where you would run your expanding enterprise."

The fisherman asked, "But how long will all this take?"

The American replied, "Fifteen to twenty years."

"But what then?"

The American laughed and said, "That's the best part. When the time is right you would announce an IPO and sell your company stock to the public and become very rich; you would make millions."

"Millions...then what?"

The American said, "Then you would retire. You could move to a small coastal fishing village where you would sleep late, fish a little, play with your kids, take a siesta with your wife, and in the evenings stroll to the village, where you could sip wine and play your guitar with your amigos."

We've been fed so many Big Fat Lies about success. Let's look at them on one by one, and let's get to work on getting your meaning back!

BIG FAT LIE #21

I feel overwhelmed.

The Truth: Whenever I hear people utter this Lie, I always suspect that something else is going on. Most of the time when we feel overwhelmed, we're actually *under*whelmed. We feel overwhelmed when we fill our lives with activities and tasks that feel empty, when we do things that we don't actually value, or when we've lost connection with our inspiration and desires. In other words, we are *under*whelmed by the things in our lives that hold no meaning. And that just sucks!

When your Inner Mean Girl looks around and sees a schedule filled with tedious, *under*whelming tasks that are disconnected from inspiration and passion, she convinces you that you're tired, inadequate, and not doing enough. You think the problem is organization or that you need more energy and time. But your Inner Wisdom knows that you can challenge yourself to make choices that are downright thrilling. When was the last time you heard someone who was deeply living her dream say she felt overwhelmed? Instead, she might say, "I'm busier than I have ever been, and I'm completely energized!"

Meet Sue, the mother of two small children and the owner of a home-based business who found herself in a constant state of overwhelm. Her schedule was hectic, and she felt she barely had time to sleep or eat. This working mom looked like she would cry if so much as a pea fell off her plate. After a few months of coaching, we unraveled the truth: Sue disliked about 75 percent of all tasks required to make her home-based business operate successfully. She was *under*whelmed because she had lost any connection to her passion and life purpose. The minute Sue was willing to be honest, her spirits began to rise.

We discussed options that were more in line with her interests, and Sue decided on a new career path. Even though she needed to work longer hours during the transition, Sue felt invigorated by her passion and actually looked forward to work (imagine that!). This sense of connection eliminated her feeling of overwhelm and allowed her to feel much more joyful. And, of course, she became more successful in every aspect of her life as well. Her Inner Critic, whom we dubbed Overwhelmed Olga, transformed from a bully who overpowered her to a pest who merely whispered to Sue on her off days.

Challenge: You don't need to change your whole career in order to feel less overwhelmed. Instead, use the Choose, Lose, or Delegate system to put yourself on the road to a more energizing and inspiring life. Start by creating a list of all the weekly or monthly activities that make you feel overwhelmed. Then, sort them by using these three categories: Choose, Lose, and Delegate.

- *Choose:* These activities are the ones that make you feel satisfied — the ones that you claim with a sense of enthusiasm and purpose. We'll call this state of mind "being at choice."

- *Lose:* These are the things you're doing that simply don't need to be done — the ones that you dislike and are willing to let go of entirely.
- *Delegate:* These activities are those that you dislike doing and that you can delegate to someone else.

For example, you may have the following tasks on your monthly list:

- Take your kids to their weekly art class — Choose. You love seeing your kids in class, so you make the decision to be 100 percent present while they create their masterpieces.
- Balance the checkbook and pay the bills — Choose. Although you feel less than enthusiastic about this task, you don't want your partner to do it (he or she isn't great with numbers!), and you don't have the means to hire an accountant at this time. You recognize that you really value having your money in order. Inspired by what you'll gain, you decide to stop feeling victimized and to reclaim this task with a sense of purpose and power. You are now "at choice."
- Get your nails done — Lose. You decide that you actually don't love getting your nails done. It takes thirty minutes to get to the salon, and the results don't last all that long. You like luxury, but you also like flow. This may be a treat that's actually costing you momentum right now. You decide to take this one off your list for the time being.
- Vacuum and dust your house each month — Delegate. Doing this yourself turns out to be really time consuming, and it zaps your energy for other more important

activities. You decide to hire or barter for a housekeeper or to delegate the task to your partner.

Affirmation: I choose how I spend my days and how I spend my life. I feel balanced, connected, and empowered.

> *"How we spend our days is how we spend our lives."*
> — ANNIE DILLARD, Pulitzer Prize–winning American author

I'm a failure.

The Truth: Human beings fail. In fact, we all fail all the time. Winston Churchill put it brilliantly when he said, "Success is leaping from failure to failure without loss of enthusiasm."

The problem is that when we fail, we tend to believe that we've become *failures*. In reality, we just *experienced* failure — that's it. Failures are opportunities for reflection, growth, maturity, and wisdom. After all, failure is a part of life — no matter how successful you are. Check out these stats:

- Babe Ruth had 1,330 career strikeouts.
- At one point, Donald Trump had $900 million in personal debt and four years of repeated failure and financial ruin.
- Oprah Winfrey's movie *Beloved* was a box office bust, losing approximately $30 million.

But these aren't the stories we remember most or even pay attention to, right? The truth is that the road to success is paved with failures. It isn't in avoiding failures that we achieve success, but in *processing* our failures effectively.

Challenge: Write down a list of all your failures over the past year. Next to each failure, write down how it helped you grow. In other words, what did you learn about yourself and about life? Make sure to phrase your learning in a positive way. In other words, instead of saying, "I learned that I suck at accounting" try phrasing it "I learned that delegation is key to my success."

Take a look. Did failing the bar exam lead you to a better understanding of how to study? Did failing in your marriage allow you to learn how to stand up and love yourself above all else? Did failing to meet your budget on a project teach you how to negotiate better? Transform your failures into learning and opportunities for growth, and your Big Fat Lies will fade into the background.

Affirmation: Like all successful people, I leap from failure to failure without any loss of enthusiasm, and I learn more and more each time.

"You may have a fresh start any moment you choose,
for this thing we call 'failure' is not the falling down,
but the staying down."
— MARY PICKFORD, Canadian-American actress
and cofounder of United Artists Film Studio

> *If I keep racing,*
> *I'll finally catch up.*

The Truth: We'll never get "it" done. The moment we check off one item on the to-do list, a new item appears. Need proof? Clean out your email in-box and breathe a sigh of relief. Within five minutes another email is sure to come in.

Change is the only constant in life, the only thing we can count on. The notion that someday we will actually get everything done is ludicrous. Instead, we need to focus on our journey and find joy in just being alive.

I remind myself and my clients all the time that with life comes a never-ending to-do list. There will always be more to get done. The real thing to focus on is what you *want* to do. Then you can do it and enjoy the journey. The idea that racing around is helpful is a myth. Slow down, take a breath, and smell the roses!

Challenge: Knowing that life comes with a never-ending to-do list, the key to everyday joy is adopting a positive mind-set about your incomplete items. Get your power back by declaring how you will be with the undone things in your life. Feeling rushed, overly busy, and stressed is a *choice*.

What perspective are you willing to adopt for the next thirty days about your busy life and your never-ending to-do list? Fill in the blank with a positive adverb that you aspire to: I'm _____ busy. For example, I'm joyfully busy. I'm delightfully busy. I'm whimsically busy. Decide to make this your new story about your schedule and your to-do list, and collect proof of its truth. If you decided on the perspective "I'm magically busy," bring your attention to how magic appears in your life. Did your sweetie come home with take-out for dinner on a night when you really didn't feel like cooking? Did you magically get an extension on the deadline you were stressed about? Did your child come home and announce that the fund-raiser had been rescheduled — for a time that works way better for you? Drink in the magic of your new perspective!

Affirmation: Use your new "busy" description as your affirmation!

*"As busy as I claim to be,
I've still got the greatest job in the world."*

— PETER CRISS, American rock star, drummer of KISS

I'm supposed to be farther along.

Can also show up as:

I'm at the wrong place
at the wrong time.

The Truth: You are always at the right place at the right time. There is no other version of you that is having a perfect experience — there is only *you* in this very moment having this very experience. So why would you want to label your experience "wrong"?

Now, don't misunderstand me; we all have moments that feel bad and experiences that tempt us to name the time and place as wrong. Yet, when we look back on those dark times with our twenty-twenty hindsight, it seems we can always find the reason that we needed to experience what we did, when we did. We needed to grow in order to give birth to our new desires and experiences.

You have the freedom to assign meaning to your life. You are the meaning maker. Without your dark experiences, you would not appreciate the joyful times nearly as much. The dark times in your life allow you to become stronger — they give you character and depth.

So throw away your "wrong" labels and start labeling your experiences as "right." Why would you spend time worrying about where you are supposed to be when you could be appreciating where you are? Be grateful for past lessons, and keep your attention on the present.

The other day I coached a client who was allowing her Inner Mean Girl to torture her with the idea that she was supposed to be farther along. Marie felt like a failure, believing she should have a better career, be making more money. Her Inner Critic was yelling, "You're almost fifty years old; your life is supposed to look so much *better* than this." (And boy, haven't we all heard that voice inside our heads? That Inner Mean Girl can be so *mean*!)

But when Marie took a deep breath and tuned in to her Inner Wisdom, she was able to see how far along she really was.

- She was able to look at her divorce as a teacher, one that made her stronger and helped create the beautiful, spirited woman she is today.
- She was able to acknowledge that putting her career on a slower path had allowed her to spend more time with her kids, who are the sunshine of her life.
- She understood that she was right where she was supposed to be, and she said she felt like she could breathe again — that in letting go of that old belief, she felt suddenly liberated and energized.
- She really accepted that she is at the right place at the right time. She always has been and always will be.

Marie looked at the big picture of her life and was able to express gratitude for *all* her experiences.

Challenge: Throw out those old measuring sticks and rulers! Get clear about where you are *truly* supposed to be by answering the questions below.

- Picture your life as it was ten years ago. Where did you feel you were supposed to be at that time?
- What does your present-day self have to say to your past self?
- How much do you wish you had simply appreciated where you were ten years ago (and how fabulous you looked)?
- Now imagine yourself ten years in the future looking back on your present-day self. What does your future self have to say to you? What is she wishing you'd appreciate more?

Affirmation: I am always at the right place at the right time.

"One day, in retrospect, the years of struggle will strike you as the most beautiful."

— SIGMUND FREUD,
Austrian neurologist and the founder of psychoanalysis

The only way I'll ever get anywhere is with hard work.

The Truth: Difficulty is not a prerequisite for success. Hard work can get you places, but so can ease-filled, inspired action. Although success may require discipline and focus, it is not predicated on a prescribed amount of discomfort or pain. In truth, if you feel you are working super-duper hard and swimming against the current, that may be a sign that you're headed in the wrong direction.

Really, haven't you ever noticed that when you feel inspired, work doesn't feel like work at all? When your beliefs match your desires, your work will feel worthwhile and fun. You will feel carried by the current as you cruise down the river to your inspired destination. And, boy, what a difference inspired work makes in terms of results.

I'll never forget an actress client of mine named Jessica who desperately wanted to find a good agent. Getting a top agent in LA is no easy feat, especially if you take the road of hard work instead of inspired action. At the time, one of the most common ways actors went about getting agents was by mailing out their head-shots and résumés. To do this, they spent a lot of time, money, and energy. Then the actors would wait anxiously for a phone call from an agent saying, "Okay, I want to meet you and perhaps represent you." My goodness, I get exhausted just thinking about it! Unfortunately, 90 percent of the time no calls came in and the envelopes ended up in a pile in an agent's office, in the trash, or on the never-to-be-opened pile. Jessica thought she needed to earn an agent through all this hard work — hard work that might not even net her a meeting. Finally, I told her, "As your coach, I will not let you do this!" I asked her what she felt inspired to do. Her Inner Wisdom's answer: to teach her exercise class and per-form in a play. She did just that, and guess what? An agent she adored ended up becoming a regular in her exercise class, saw her in the play, and asked her to be her client! How's that for inspired action producing great results?

Of course, Jessica worked to perform the agent-winning role. She also worked to create her successful exercise class. However, this was happy, purpose-filled work that she enjoyed. Work that is energized in this way cannot help but attract connections and outcomes that feel good. Great results often come from feeling great to begin with!

Challenge: To stop believing this Lie, answer the following ques-tions about a situation in which you are working too hard with-out seeing results:

- Is it true that hard work always pays off in this situation? In other words, if you are working hard at finding a soul-mate by tirelessly scouring dating websites, is there any guarantee that your efforts will pay off?
- Can you think of someone who has succeeded because of an amazing coincidence or a stroke of good luck,

someone like Jessica? If it's possible for one person, it's possible for you too.

- Let your imagination run wild creating a stroke-of-luck story for yourself. Really have fun imagining all the crazy details from beginning to end. ("I've decided to go skiing to distract myself from this whole online dating thing. While I'm happily be-bopping down the slopes, I meet a smart, charming eleven-year-old girl and give her a few tips on her form. It turns out her single father is smart, funny, sincere, and perfect for me, and he adores me instantly. Six months later we get married on the bunny slope!")

Affirmation: Even my work feels like play because I follow my inspirations.

"When you feel like you are swimming upstream, just flip over and float."

— TERRI COLE, American psychotherapist, life coach, author, and motivational speaker

*Focusing on my problems
helps me solve them.*

The Truth: Whatever we focus on grows. Haven't you ever noticed this phenomenon? Focus on the color blue surrounding you right now. Look around the room and notice all the blue. Decide that blue is important and watch as your mind (the reticular activating system in your brain to be exact) brings all things blue into your line of vision. It is as if all the blue in the room just grew!

So if you have a challenge or problem you're ready to solve, stop focusing on the problem, start focusing on the solution, and watch the possibilities expand. It is so easy to fall into the trap of focusing so strongly on the challenges in our lives that we cannot see anything else. It is vital to gain clarity by focusing on what you want instead of on your problems.

Rebecca was a vibrant saleswoman who came to me with overwhelming financial problems. She was in the midst of a true crisis: creditors were constantly calling, and her car was almost repossessed. Talk about a focus challenge! It was extremely difficult for her *not* to focus on her financial worries, especially since they were constantly being shoved in her face. I asked her to try looking at the big picture of her life. From this meta-view, she was able to analyze the pattern of her financial irresponsibility: not only how it all started, but also how she could solve it. She made a commitment to solving her money issues by entering a debt consolidation program and downsizing to a smaller home, steps that allowed her to free up equity and climb out of her hole. She was debt free within three years and hasn't looked back since! And it all began by focusing on the solutions and allowing them to mushroom.

Challenge: Make a list of three challenges you face. Now imagine that you are in a helicopter high up in the air, far above them all. Watch as your problems begin to fade until they are mere dots on the ground. Notice what you can see from this vantage point. Look where you're headed. Look to the land of solution. Look to the land of desire. Now look at your list of challenges. Write down at least two possible solutions for every issue, and challenge yourself to stay focused on what you want instead of on the challenge itself.

Affirmation: I see my solutions expand like the blue in the room!

*"We cannot solve our problems
with the same thinking we used when we created them."*
— ALBERT EINSTEIN, German-born physicist

BIG FAT LIE #27

I'll try.

The Truth: Trying is not good enough; you need to commit. I cringe whenever I hear my clients use the word *try* because I know it means they are skirting true commitment.

Here's a litmus test you can use to see just how committed you really are. Paul, a member of one of my coaching groups, kept putting off finishing the first draft of his book. Week after week, he would come to the coaching session without hitting his deadline. At the end of the group, I decided to challenge him. When I asked him what he was committing to, he told me he planned to complete his first draft before the next group meeting. I then asked him if he was willing to donate $150 to a political organization to which he was *diametrically opposed* if he showed up to the next group without completing his commitment. He argued with me, protesting that there was no way he would give money to an organization he didn't believe in. Fabulous! At last he was able to see how noncommittal he was about finishing his book. By the end of our session, Paul rose to the challenge, and — of course — showed up at the next group with the first draft of his book complete.

Challenge: Next time you hear yourself saying "I'll try," analyze what you're not committing to by answering the following questions:

1. Do you truly want to commit? Pause here and ask yourself if this commitment matches up with your desire.

2. Are you setting yourself up for failure? So often we use the whole "I'll try" story to punish ourselves, perpetuating the "I'm a loser" story. Yuck!

3. Are you committing out of obligation? Listen, I'm a mom and know a thing or two about making commitments out of obligation — think fund-raisers and play dates. I've had to get really clear about the commitments I'm making so that my word means something both to me and to others. I say either, "Yes, I will do that" or "No, not this time," instead of the "I'll try" side-stepping dance. Join me in the Truth-Telling Revolution!

4. What do you know you can commit to? Maybe you can't head up the committee, but perhaps you're happy to help set up for the big event. Get clear on what you are ready to commit to.

5. Now, revise and commit to something that you are truly ready to take on. In other words, you've officially shifted from "I'll try" to "I commit." Doesn't that feel better?

6. Finally, test yourself. Are you willing to eat your least favorite food if you don't follow through? Would you

donate to a cause you don't believe in? If not, go back to question 5 and revise your commitment until you pass the litmus test.

Affirmation: Write your own affirmation here, using one of your "I will" statements from above.

> *"Try not. Do…or do not. There is no try."*
> — YODA, intergalactic Jedi master, from *Star Wars*

If I allow myself to celebrate, the other shoe will drop.

Can also show up as:

If I get too happy, something bad will happen.

The Truth: When you stop yourself from celebrating, you rob yourself of joy. Believing that being too happy or receiving too many good things means you are due for a disaster is truly twisted thinking. It is like having a police force dedicated to creating fear inside your head.

I always chuckle when people tell me they are "trying not to get too excited" about something or when they say, "I don't know if I should tell you because I might jinx it." Get excited! Celebrate your successes (and even the possibility of success!) simply for the *joy* of celebration in the moment. Why not? You truly have nothing to lose! Even if things don't turn out as you expect, wouldn't you rather have been happy than never to have celebrated at all?

And when you've reached a level of happiness and success that you're overjoyed with, please, for the love of God (really, truly, God/the universe/source energy wants you to be happy), relish it! It is blasphemous to deny your joy. It is your birthright to feel happy. Inspire others with your joy. Be the sunshine in the world and savor every moment. You deserve it!

Let's take a cue from two-year-olds. I remember when my daughter was two years old and *celebrated everything*. This is one of my favorite things about being Annabella's mom. Drinking a smoothie? Clap your hands with glee. Made it up the stairs all by yourself? Shout with joy, "I did it!" Have a friend coming over to play? Run around and do the happy dance! Couldn't we all celebrate more? Isn't it wonderful when we acknowledge our wins? Let's take this tip from Annabella and start noticing and focusing on our wins and on when we feel *good*. Relish your joy!

Challenge: Make a list of all the things you have yet to celebrate. Is there a possible promotion in your future? Ride the wave of excitement *now*, just for fun! Is there a new beau who could be "the one"? Why not celebrate it as if it has already happened just for the joy of it? Find a way to formally celebrate potential successes, as well as concrete wins. Mark such occasions: go out for a celebration dinner, brag to your mom, send yourself flowers, or simply take a bubble bath. Life is too short not to celebrate!

Now let's drive it home with this exercise:

- Think of a time when you really felt on top of the world, a peak experience, a time when you allowed yourself to relish the joy of the moment.
- As you make a detailed picture in your mind of that memory, check in with yourself and ask: What were you feeling about the future in that moment? A readiness to conquer the world? A sense of joyful possibility? A feeling that all was right with the world? Most people report that in their peak memories they felt joyful, powerful, and excited about their future. Let's put it this way: I've

never seen a person getting married, accepting an Olympic medal, or taking in a standing ovation look worried about when the other shoe will drop, have you?

• Notice that when you deeply allow yourself to celebrate joy, you generate more joy.

Affirmation: I celebrate even the *hint* of good news, because I know that joy begets more joy!

"Nothing is so contagious as enthusiasm:
it moves stones, it charms brutes.
Enthusiasm is the genius of sincerity,
and truth accomplishes no victories without it."

— EDWARD BULWER-LYTTON,
English politician and playwright

I gotta pay my dues.

The Truth: What if all your dues were paid in full? What if it was your birthright to enjoy everything your heart desires? I know it may sound irreverent, but the truth is, we don't need to pay our dues, and those who tell you otherwise are usually referring to the path they've had to walk themselves. You can be one of the lucky ones: good things can happen magically in your life. How yummy is that?

Siena thought that she had to pay her dues and climb the ladder one rung at a time. She felt like it was cheating to take quantum leaps. After all, she came from a practical family that had instilled a hardcore work ethic. And it had gotten her places. The problem was that she wasn't happy, and she wanted to switch gears from being a lawyer in a big firm, where she was slowly working her way up, to starting her own firm with a trusted colleague who had landed a big account that would pave the way for the new firm. That's when her Inner Critic stepped in to tell her that she needed to pay her dues and that there was no way she was ready for this opportunity. It felt too lucky, too charmed, too magical to walk into such a sweet deal.

As Siena's coach I knew what my mission was: to get the "I gotta pay my dues" Lie out of Siena's path to success. Through our work we uncovered how much this perspective had sabotaged her success in the past. She was ready to lay it to rest and become one of the lucky ones. Siena started to feel like her dues were paid in full and that she could attract success, opportunities, and luck to herself. She made the leap, and the new firm took off like gangbusters!

Challenge: Uncover your "gotta pay my dues" beliefs by answering the following statements with true or false:

- I must earn everything I get. (If you answered true, take a note from Siena and see how you can shift your focus to attracting success as opposed to earning it.)
- I resent people who have things handed to them. (If you answered true, begin to notice how this is blocking you from having things handed to you. Get inspired when others have good luck. Then claim what you want by saying, "I'm ready for x to be handed to me on a silver platter!")
- Some people are lucky and some aren't, and I am one of the unlucky ones. (If you answered true, then start to collect evidence of your luck. Make a "lucky list" and feel how charmed your life really has been. We all have places in our life where we feel lucky. Maybe you're lucky in love? Lucky with money? Lucky with finding great deals on shoes? Lucky in friendships?)
- It is okay for me to receive unearned things. (If you answered false, then I challenge you to make a point to gracefully receive — starting today. Receive a compliment

that feels unearned. Receive a few pounds lost when you weren't even trying. Receive a new friend's invitation to the ballet. Just receive — no questions asked!)

• Taking a shortcut is cheating. (If you answered true, then it is time for you to bless the shortcuts in your life. Start with baby ones such as a shortcut through the line on the freeway or having your assistant do the first edits on your report...anything that makes you say, "Can I really *do* that?")

Notice where your beliefs are sabotaging your joy and success. Then try the affirmation below, and see how things shift.

Affirmation: I hereby declare that my dues are paid in full, and I allow luck, ease, and grace into my life.

> *"Who told you that you had to make the best*
> *of a bad situation?...*
> *You don't have to pay any more dues."*
>
> — CHELLIE CAMPBELL, American author, speaker,
> and financial stress-reduction specialist

*If I don't know how,
I can't have it.*

Can also show up as:

*In order to achieve my goals,
I need to know how I'll get there.*

The Truth: In order to succeed, you need to identify what you desire and believe you can get it. After you have a clear vision of where you want to go and truly believe that you can get there, then you can begin to take inspired actions that feel joyful and intuitively right. The *how* question often stops us from dreaming. Take your foot off the *how* pedal and step on the *desire* pedal instead. Let yourself dream, and watch yourself fly!

Picture this: I was sitting with my baby girl, who was about nine months old, when I got a call from the termite company informing us that we had about $25,000 worth of unexpected work that needed to be done on the house we had just bought. The exact phrase was, "The stucco is holding up the entire side of the house." Add to that a business partnership of seven years that was in the midst of dissolving. Gulp. Boy, was this an intense, challenging time! Despite the circumstances, I had a crazy inkling that I had a great idea on my hands. I wanted to bring women together on a tele-series to give them access to all the female luminaries I admired most, such as Marianne Williamson, Marci Shimoff, SARK, and Lisa Nichols. I had been reading and learning from these women for more than fifteen years. I had the vision, all right, but I had no idea of *how* I was going to execute it.

So I did what I often do when I'm at a loss for how I'm going to make it all work: I left Annabella at home with her amazing dad and went on a run in the hills with my mutt, Dozer. At the beginning of the run, I set the intention to gain clarity and a plan. I ran hard and fast and allowed inspiration to bubble up. By the end of the run, I had a name for the series and my next action step. The Women Masters Tele-Seminar Series was born, and I began by simply emailing all the experts I admired most, telling them my vision and inviting them on to the series. I went to websites and filled out contact forms — not letting my doubt or Inner Mean Girl stop me. The result? My entire life changed...I became friends with many of the masters...I tripled my income ...I began having the impact I wanted to have in the world...and ultimately I landed this book deal. If I had let my Inner Critic's incessant *how* questions (How are you going to do that? How will you reach these experts? How are you going to build a website? How will the technology work?) stop me, you wouldn't be reading this book today. (Plus, the termites would have eaten my house!) Take it from me: it begins with a desire and a vision and then taking that first inspired step. The rest will reveal itself. (Want to hear a few Women Masters interviews? Log on to www .BigFatLiesTheBook.com to grab your reader's tool kit, which includes some of my favorite Women Masters interviews for free!)

Challenge:
- Begin by committing to ten minutes of dreaming and visioning time to explore what you most desire. No *how* questions allowed!

- Really flesh out your vision. What does it look like? Feel like? What impact are you having on the world? Allow yourself to dream big.
- Then set the intention and go on whatever your version of a run is to turn off your Big Fat Lies chatter. You might take a long bath, knit a scarf, go on a hike, state your intention before a good night's sleep (your unconscious mind can work out an action plan in your sleep, lickety-split!), or sit in front of a nearby body of water, letting the crashing waves or the stillness of the water wash over you, helping you to fulfill your intention.
- Your mission is to really allow your inspiration and intention to guide you. You only need to know the next step, not *all* the steps, to begin!
- Discover what the next inspired step is, and go for it.

Affirmation: I trust my vision, use inspiration as my guide, and know that the "how" will gracefully unfold.

> *"Obstacles are those frightful things you see*
> *when you take your eyes off your goal."*
> — HENRY FORD, American industrialist
> and founder of the Ford Motor Company

BIG FAT LIES ABOUT MONEY

*M*oney. *The very word inspires dreams,* nightmares, even songs. (I've got one famous money song running through my head right now — can you hum one now too?) We give money so much power and meaning. We perpetually want more and simultaneously feel scared, overwhelmed, or guilty when we do have more. The push and pull of money in our lives is daunting, and the topic is infused with Big Fat Lies.

But another possibility is brewing. And I can't think of a finer example than my friend Mary, a smart-as-a-whip, pint-size businesswoman and practicing Buddhist who has a beautifully balanced relationship with money. She pays herself first by contributing to her savings and retirement accounts before spending on other things mindlessly. In this way she expresses her faith in a prosperous future. She sets up separate savings accounts for special, high-end expenses such as renovating her kitchen or going on a three-month retreat in the Himalayas. She embarks on those big projects with a big smile, since they have been fully funded in advance. She always gives 10 percent of her net profit to worthy causes, people who inspire her, and organizations she believes in. In fact, she once surprised me with a $100 tithe for just being me. How blown away and delighted was I? (Very!) And while she's not above the occasional splurge, she pays off her credit cards in full every month.

For Mary, the discipline of managing her money is the same as the discipline of her meditation practice: she doesn't expect herself to do everything perfectly all the time, but abiding to a consistent, daily commitment gives her both structure and freedom. Mary has imbued money with a meaning that works for her. She believes that money flows, that she always has more than enough, and that money is merely one facet of her life. In other words, her bank account is not tied to her self-worth.

Our Inner Wisdom and Inner Superstar know that we can be just like Mary. We can marry spirituality with wealth and keep our happiness separate from our bank account balance. So let's dive into the murky money waters together and come back up again, shining bright!

Money is the root of all evil.

Can also show up as:

*Rich people are greedy and bad.
Money causes nothing
but problems and conflict.*

The Truth: When you have negative thoughts or feelings about money, you are subconsciously holding yourself apart from wealth. You don't want to become something that you judge as wrong or bad, yet at the same time you want more wealth and abundance. You are in a push-pull relationship with money, in one breath saying you desperately want it and in the next breath condemning it. It's as if money has become some horrible boyfriend who is just not that into you! These mixed messages will keep you in a holding pattern. It's time to clean up your money relationship and beliefs, so that you can both attract more of it *and* stop giving it the power to make you unhappy, miserable, and victimized.

Janet, a gifted hair and makeup artist, consistently found herself in financial turmoil. As we talked about money, we uncovered that she had some very deep-seated negative beliefs and fears about wealth. She realized that, in her mind, having money and being wealthy equaled being a spoiled, uncaring, heartless person. Once we untangled her fears and beliefs, we began to smooth them out and transform them into positive beliefs that moved her closer to her true self. Her Inner Wisdom told her to ingrain this new belief: "The more money I make, the more I contribute to the world." She began to focus on stories of wealthy public figures who are making a positive difference. She noticed that as she collected evidence to support the notion that wealth is a positive force, she created more money in her life. She received a raise at her job, cleaned up her credit score, paid down her debt, and began a savings account. She even began donating 5 percent of her income to her favorite charity. This was a life-changing perspective shift for her, and I'm happy to report that she continues to believe that wealth is a good thing and continues to create more and more abundance in her life.

Challenge: Take charge of your relationship with money by paying attention to your beliefs about how it's created, lost, and multiplied. Follow the six-step process below:

- Assess how money is usually handled in your family. Is it revered? Taken for granted? Constantly being chased? Treated as evil and bad?
- In what ways do you feel rich? Take a moment to appreciate the abundance that is already present in your life. Maybe you have an abundance of friends, of great power suits, of family, of energy, of humor?
- Take a look at your relationship with money. When someone brings up the topic, how do you react? Is there a knot in your stomach? A smile on your face?

- Decide to create a new relationship with money by writing out how you'd like to feel about it. Ask your Inner Wisdom for her advice on what money belief would best serve you.

- Make a perspective chain about money. (This exercise was inspired by the words and work of Abraham-Hicks.) Write the numbers 1 through 7 on a piece of paper. In the #1 spot write the current perspective you hold about money. The #7 spot represents the Inner Wisdom perspective you'd most like to hold about money. Then begin to fill in the middle with perspectives that will link your current perspective to the perspective you'd like to hold. You'll have a perspective plan to help you work your way to your ideal money perspective. Here's a money sample perspective chain:

  1. Money is the root of all evil.
  2. Not all money comes from bad people.
  3. Money is merely a source of energy.
  4. I like it when I have plenty of money.
  5. There are times when I've had money.
  6. It is possible for me to create more money.
  7. Money is on its way to me.

- The final step is to live each perspective for a day. Begin with the #1 perspective (which will be quite easy since it is your current perspective, which you know oh-so-well!). Collect evidence of why that perspective is accurate. The next day step into the #2 perspective and amplify its volume and truth, building a case to support it. Continue until you end on the #7 perspective about money, the perspective you'd like to hold. Within seven days you will be living your ideal perspective. Watch joy (and money!) flow in.

Affirmation: Fill in your perspective chain to use as affirmations for the next week!

"Bless that which you want."

— HUNA PHILOSOPHY

*If I only had enough money,
everything would be okay.*

Can also show up as:

When I'm rich, then I'll be happy.

The Truth: Now that we've started to transform our negative beliefs about money, let's ensure that we don't fall into the Big Fat Lie that says you need money to be happy. Money is simply one source of commerce that allows us to live a certain material lifestyle. And the idea that money will take care of all our worries? Ha! According to the Certified Financial Planner Board of Standards, nearly a third of all lottery winners become bankrupt and claim that the winnings caused more trouble than good.

When we collapse "having money" with "having happiness" we set ourselves up for disappointment and ultimately powerlessness. And feeling frustrated and impotent actually makes it harder to create money. What a cycle to be in!

Challenge: Take a look at the big picture of your finances and of your happiness and how they do or don't correlate. Make a chart reflecting the past ten years. In that chart, one line will represent happiness, the other line finances. Rate on a satisfaction scale of 1 to 10 (1 = horrible, 5 = medium, 10 = fabulous) your happiness and finances at each time period:

- Now: How do you rate your happiness (1 to 10)? Your finances (1 to 10)?
- 2 years ago: How would you rate your happiness (1 to 10)? Your finances (1 to 10)?
- 7 years ago: How would you rate your happiness (1 to 10)? Your finances (1 to 10)?
- 10 years ago: How would you rate your happiness (1 to 10)? Your finances (1 to 10)?

Then chart your results, so you have a visual representation. Here is a sample:

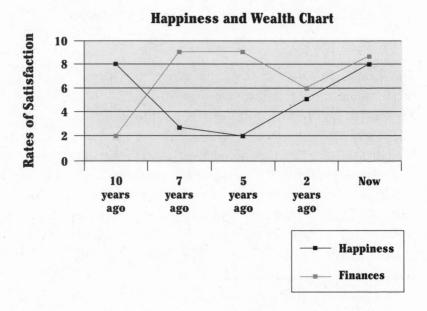

Answer the following:

- What do you notice? Does your happiness truly correlate with your finances?

- When did you have both happiness and financial abundance? What do you attribute that to? Really take note here of what worked well during that time period. This is a golden time when your Inner Superstar was shining bright. Make a list of what was present that made possible such a wonderful period of abundance and happiness.

Affirmation: As I move through my life, I joyfully nurture both my finances and my happiness.

> *"Success is not a place at which one arrives*
> *but rather the spirit with which one undertakes*
> *and continues the journey."*
> — ALEX NOBLE, French-American writer

I'll never have enough.

The Truth: As we've discussed, it is part of the human experience to constantly desire more. However, let us not confuse that with feeling as if we don't have enough. It's imperative that you find a way to make peace with where you are in life right now and to enjoy the journey itself.

Have you ever gone hiking and reached the top of the mountain, only to find that there was another mountain peak to climb, one that was out of view until you reached a certain height? That is exactly how life is: there will always be more mountains to climb, but we can approach the trek with joy, enthusiasm, and grace. Celebrate your milestones as the accomplishments they are, and relish how much you have!

Challenge: Where do you want to go next? What will make it possible for you to enjoy the climb to the next peak? Try the following exercise to gear up for a joyful journey:

- Write down what you currently see from your vantage point. Make a list of everything you appreciate about the state of your life.
- Next, make a list of where you want to go next. What do you believe is waiting for you at the next logical peak?
- What do you imagine you will appreciate more at the next peak than you do at your current vantage point?
- Make the decision to deliberately begin appreciating those things right now, as if you already had them.
- Put a sticky note on your mirror or in your car that reminds you of the gifts that await you at the next milestone.
- Finally, enjoy the climb up!

Affirmation: On this joyful journey of my life, I have more than enough and am eager to have more!

> *"When we let go of the chase for more,*
> *and consciously examine and experience the resources*
> *we already have, we discover our resources are deeper*
> *than we knew or imagined. In the nourishment*
> *of our attention, our assets expand and grow."*

— LYNNE TWIST, American activist, speaker, and author, founder of the Soul of Money Institute

BIG FAT LIE #34

I am one of the have-nots.

Can also show up as:

I don't deserve money.
I am destined to be broke forever.

The Truth: No one declared you a "have-not" at birth. In fact, it is your *birthright* to have a life filled with joy and happiness and money. Really absorb that for a moment. Would a higher power bring you into this world just to make you struggle?

The key is to stop perpetuating this Lie and stop going to extremes — that is the land where your Inner Critic lives. It can be easy to turn an unpaid bill into "I'm destined to be broke forever" if you're not being mindful and tuning in to your Inner Wisdom. So I want you to stop collecting evidence of how things never go your way and how undeserving you are. Instead, let's collect evidence of what your Inner Superstar knows to be true.

Challenge: Take a piece of paper and create four columns. In the left-hand column write down your top ten worst fears about money and your life. These are the self-limiting beliefs that are running rampant through your mind. In the next column, ask yourself "How much risk is there for this coming true?" This puts your Inner Mean Girl on notice! In the next column, list all evidence to the contrary. Finally, record your new Inner Superstar belief.

Here is a sample abbreviated chart:

Worst Fear	Risk of Coming True?	Evidence to the Contrary	Inner Superstar Belief
I'll always struggle with money.	Not possible.	I have always made ends meet. I have family and/or friends who would lend me money in a bind.	I always have a steady stream of money.
Dying alone, broke and unloved.	Very little risk.	I have amazing friends, I have a sister who loves me, and I have long-term-care insurance.	I will transition to the next life surrounded by loved ones and will leave behind a legacy.

Affirmation: It is my birthright to be happy and wealthy.

> *"The shortcut to anything you want in your life is to be and feel happy now! It is the fastest way to bring money and anything else you want into your life."*

— RHONDA BYRNE,
creator of the movie and book *The Secret*

It's fine to spend more than I have.

Can also show up as:

I'll just put this on my credit card and pay it off later.

The Truth: I'm all for positive thinking and manifesting by focusing on what works in life, but that doesn't mean that I advocate for financial irresponsibility or denial. There is a dance between visioning for your financial future while attracting more wealth and being awake to the truth of your financial picture with grace and accountability. This balance leads to more happiness, more money, and more confidence.

Our addiction to racking up debt has been so tragically mirrored by the U.S. government. The buy-now-pay-later mentality has gotten us into a heap of trouble. As of this writing, our national debt is up to more than *14 trillion dollars* and rising each day. Gulp…

I've played this out in my own life. I've racked up the credit card debt and lied to myself about the mismatch of how much money I was bringing in and how much money I was spending.

I've been financially disorganized and hidden from the truth of my financial picture. I've made mistakes, dug myself out of holes, and declared "No more!" And I want to inspire you to do the same.

Challenge: I had an incredible, inspiring conversation about this Big Fat Lie with my dear friend and colleague, the Reverend Karen Russo. (Make sure to go to www.BigFatLiesTheBook.com to get her Women Masters interview in your reader's tool kit for free.) She is the award-winning author of *The Money Keys*, and she has generously allowed me to share one of her fabulous money exercises with you:

- Take one aspect of your financial life that is very charged for you and turn it into a blessing. Maybe it is something that you neglect, ignore, or always procrastinate doing, such as balancing your checkbook, paying bills, or donating.
- Now decide to make that burden a sacred practice. Make it an act of self-care to be financially responsible. For example, if balancing your checkbook feels like a burden and therefore you avoid doing it, put on your favorite song, light a candle, say a prayer, and dive in. Or if you have been putting off calling your credit card companies to negotiate a lower interest rate, put on your favorite Inner Superstar heels, light some incense, say an affirmation, and dial.

This exercise is about you shifting your mind-set from thinking of money as a burden to regarding it as a blessing. As you do so, miracles will occur.

Affirmation: I love and respect myself enough to be financially responsible.

*"Many spiritual seekers feel that money is
somehow un-spiritual.
To stay 'pure,' they 'don't care about money'
and purity becomes poverty. It's not the Truth.
You can be spiritually and financially rich!"*

— KAREN RUSSO, author and spiritual guide to wealth creation

Image reprinted with permission from Karen Russo.

BIG FAT LIES

ABOUT LOVE AND RELATIONSHIPS

*P*ure love is the most powerful energy on the planet. Science has demonstrated its influence with research such as Dr. Masaru Emoto's fascinating work with water crystals. As documented in the book *The Hidden Messages in Water* and the movie *What the Bleep Do We Know!?* Dr. Emoto examined the impact of words and energy directed toward frozen water crystals. The results were astonishing! When sent loving energy with words such as *love, gratitude*, and *I'm sorry*, the crystals took on glorious forms. In contrast, when sent hateful energy with words such as *You fool* or *You make me sick*, the crystals took on dark, ominous shapes. Given that the majority of the human body is made up of water, can you imagine how fabulous it is when we send loving words and thoughts to ourselves (and what a horrific impact it can have when our Inner Critics send us hateful words)? Let's rid ourselves of the Big Fat Lies that block us from those loving words!

After all, love is the thing we crave most as human beings. And love comes in all forms: there's romantic love, paternal love, friendship love, sibling love, and, of course, self-love. Think about a peak experience in your life, a time that felt exactly right, a true best moment. Chances are that this experience centered on love, whether the moment was about feeling a deep sense of love for nature, source energy, or God; love for yourself; or love of another such as you would feel while giving birth to a child, falling in love with your soulmate, or feeling deeply connected to your best friend, sibling, or parent. Love was present in a profound way. This is where your Inner Superstar really comes out.

We human beings are pack animals, with the need to relate to one another for survival. Even the most introverted and solitude-seeking folks among us need relationships and love in their lives. So it is no wonder that relationships and love cause so much chaos and confusion — they are so important to us.

What you're about to read are the Biggest Fattest Lies that get in the way of receiving and giving love. Some are the most common ones, and others are the stealthiest and most insidious. Consider them the love-blocking Lies. The coaching exercises nurture a beautiful relationship with yourself and others so that you can learn to fully receive and fully give love.

Really look deep within to see which of these Lies you believe. And then do the coaching challenges so that you can break free from those Lies and tune in to the Truth. Here's what my Inner Wisdom knows as Truth: you are loved. And it is time you let that love in and let it flow back out!

BIG FAT LIE #36

I need another to complete me.

The Truth: Whether you believe you need a man, a romantic partner, or a child to complete you, you are dead wrong. *You are complete and whole all by yourself.*

It can be easy to fall prey to this Lie when we have everything from songs to poems to movies to greeting cards that indoctrinate us with the idea that we're less than complete without a partner, a child, and so on. Just think about all the romantic films that perpetuate this Lie with lines such as the omnipresent "You complete me" in *Jerry Maguire.* Or look at baby addicts such as Nadya Sulemen, better known as Octomom, who admits she craved wholeness when she gave birth to her babies. She now has fourteen children whom she struggles to care for.

I feel so blessed to have a husband and daughter I adore, but I don't believe that they complete me. I feel whole and am whole all by myself. And I know that if I hadn't done my work and claimed my wholeness, I would not have attracted such wonderful people into my life. It doesn't seem so long ago when I felt incomplete. I was living with my ex-boyfriend, and I felt that he completed me on every level. We were grossly enmeshed, and my identity felt wrapped up in him. I felt like I was whole only when I was with him and loved by him. This dynamic took a terrifying toll on my self-worth and self-esteem, especially when I finally realized that the relationship was unhealthy and that I could no longer tolerate it. I found myself alone and feeling incomplete. So I did exactly what I'm challenging you to do below to ingrain a sense of wholeness.

Challenge: Let's really bring home how whole you are by doing a powerful Marry Yourself ritual. I first learned about marrying myself by reading SARK's wonderful book *Succulent Wild Woman,* and it forever changed my life.

- First, I want you to make a list of vows you are ready to proclaim. Promise to never leave you. Promise to stop the self-abandonment cycle in your life. Vow to view yourself as whole and complete, with or without a romantic partner, child, or whoever else this Lie insists you need. This is about you declaring self-love on a profound level.
- Second, make a list of the ways you will show up for yourself. This is where you make your vows concrete, actionable, and measurable. This is how you can stay on track with your self-love commitment. Do you promise to go on a date night with yourself once a month? Will you develop a nourishing daily practice? Will you keep a journal of wins and accomplishments?
- Third, find a symbol of your commitment. This could be a ring or piece of jewelry or a heart stone or collage of you in your happiest moments — whatever symbolizes your wholeness and your pledge.

- Finally, do a marriage ritual in which you marry yourself. I did mine on a beach in Malibu with two other fabulous girlfriends who were doing the same. We all wore beautiful dresses and witnessed each other reading our vows, blessing our symbols, and celebrating our wholeness.

Affirmation: Say one of your marriage vows aloud in the mirror for the next thirty days.

> *"I don't like myself, I'm crazy about myself."*
>
> — MAE WEST, American actress and legendary sex symbol

Being by myself means being lonely.

The Truth: Being alone is *not* the same thing as being lonely. In fact, there is nothing lonelier than standing in a group of people or, worse yet, lying next to your partner and feeling alone. It's crucial to work on having a relationship with yourself that allows for alone time: space for you to simply be with yourself. Whenever I meet a client who is looking for a romantic partner, I always begin with her relationship with herself, making sure she has not confused being alone with being lonely. Once my single clients make peace with being alone, the floodgates often open, and new love flows in. The energy of self-love attracts people who will reflect that love back.

Challenge: This challenge is all about exploring how fabulous you are. Set aside some alone time dedicated to experiencing self-love. Try the following explorations:

- *Self-knowledge:* What are your opinions? Get to know your likes and dislikes. Think about current events and topics that interest you, books you've recently read, the movies you've seen, and more. Ask yourself, "What do I think about this?" and "What is my opinion?" Explore what you love and what you don't care for. Get to know yourself on an intimate level.
- *Spontaneity and being in the moment:* Give yourself a ME day and allow yourself to be in the moment by asking, "What do I want to do today?" and then following through. Perhaps you feel like taking a nap? Going to the gym for a workout? Taking a bath? Writing letters? Finishing that art project?
- *Self-appreciation:* Make a weekly list of the things you most appreciate about yourself. Allow this to become a ritual of self-love.
- *Evidence:* Collect evidence of how wonderful you are by tracking any acknowledgments and compliments you receive for a full week. Put this list in a visible spot. (Your closet? Dashboard? Bathroom mirror?)

Affirmation: I am my own best friend.

> *"We're all in this together...alone."*
> — LILY TOMLIN, American actress and comedian

*When I worry about my loved ones,
I am loving them.*

The Truth: You cannot worry about and love someone in the same moment. It is your job to *love* those you care about, not to worry about them. We often confuse these two emotions and think they're irrevocably linked, but love and worry are very near opposites. Love stems from your heart and soul, from appreciation and faith. Worry stems from fear, anxiety, and faithlessness and creates negative energy. How, then, can you possibly experience love and worry at the same time?

When my daughter, Annabella, was first born, I had to learn and practice the skill of shifting from worry to love on a day-to-day, sometimes even moment-by-moment, basis. When we first brought her home, I remember feeling anxious and having racing thoughts of worry. "Is she breathing?" "Did she get enough milk?" "Is she supposed to be sneezing so much?" I had a decision to make. Either I was going to be a fretful, anxiety-ridden, worrywart of a mom, or I was going to have to practice what

140

I preach and turn to love and faith. I learned to shut off my "worry mind" and concentrate on the love I feel for her. When I feel worry creeping in, I consciously choose to shift to love and think thoughts such as, "I love my daughter," "She is so spirited and full of life," "I love the way she laughs," "I trust that she is safe." So the next time you slip into worry, make the shift, and you'll experience the power of love for yourself.

Challenge: Think of a loved one. Allow yourself to worry about her for a moment. Notice how worrying makes you feel — maybe your chest closes up, your body shakes, your fists clench, or your pulse races. Now, shift into love. Ahhh, much better. Really pump up the love. Imagine her smile, the sweetness in her voice, the sparkle in her eyes. Notice how love inspires positive sensations — maybe a smile spread across your face, your heart opened, or your shoulders relaxed. The next time you start to worry about a loved one, shift your attention to the love you feel for him instead.

Affirmation: I transform my worries into visions of peace, strength, and love.

> *"Worrying is like a rocking chair:*
> *It gives you something to do,*
> *but it doesn't get you anywhere."*

— *National Lampoon's Van Wilder*, directed by WALT BECKER

*If you love someone,
you must be willing to sacrifice.*

The Truth: Being in service to others is a way to love them, but there's a huge difference between being *in service* and being *in sacrifice.* As I learned from leading and teaching with fellow coach Melissa McFarlane, the minute you step into the world of sacrifice, you are paving the road to resentment and anger. When, however, you are in service to someone, you are operating from a space of authentic giving and are not depleting yourself for the well-being of another (you may even feel willing to joyfully compromise). And this is what true love is.

The distinction between service and sacrifice can be subtle. It is simply a question of tuning in to your emotions, looking at how you feel, and noticing the place you are giving from. You need to know how much you can give without depleting and sacrificing yourself. Because life is constantly changing, how much you can give and be in service changes as well.

For example, if you are currently in a major life transition

142

(getting divorced, getting married, shifting careers, buying a home, having a baby, dealing with a troubled teenager), your threshold for giving may be very low. You need to focus on yourself, on giving back to you. You need to be "selfish" (see Big Fat Lie #15 on selfishness for more thoughts on this). When you are giving and feeling resentful, overwhelmed, and victimized, or if you find yourself keeping score, this is a clear sign that you are in sacrifice.

If, however, you're in a wonderful place where you feel settled, at peace, filled with inspiration and passion, you are probably ready to be in service to others. This is usually the perfect time to do volunteer work or to step up to the plate for a friend in need. When you are giving and it feels energizing, this is a clear sign that you are in service.

Challenge: Where in your life are you sacrificing? Where do you feel depleted? Make a list of all the people or situations where you are sacrificing.

For example, perhaps your mother is ill and you're run ragged trying to visit her each day. Or perhaps a friend whom you've known since high school is calling you at all hours of the night because his girlfriend left him. Now answer the following question for each situation: "What would being in service look like?"

In the case of your mother, perhaps you decide to talk to your siblings and create a Take Care of Mom schedule and cut down your visits to only twice a week. As you begin your new routine, you'll begin to notice that although your visits are less frequent, they are more meaningful. Maybe you even use some of the time you'd normally spend visiting her getting your hair done, going to the gym, or working in the garden — anything to ensure that you're operating with a full cup and authentically giving.

In the case of your friend calling you at all hours, you might decide to turn off the phone when you go to bed so that you can feel refreshed the next day and call him back when you feel you can be in service.

Create a Sacrifice-to-Service Shift Table and list the ways in which you are sacrificing. Then answer the question, What would being in service look like?

Affirmation: I love the energy that fills me when I am truly in service to others and myself.

"If I am not for myself, who will be for me?"
— RABBI HILLEL, Jewish scholar and theologian

BIG FAT LIE #40

It's all his/her/their fault.

Can also show up as:

He/she/they is/are to blame.

The Truth: It feels so much easier to blame others than to take full responsibility for your life. But life is a cocreation, and in order to create what you *do* want, you need to look at the part you've played in creating what you *don't* want. In a way, blame is a gift because it is a warning sign that you are disempowering yourself and skirting responsibility. Instead of blaming others, take a step back, reexamine your situation, and reclaim your power.

Bill used to blame his wife for all his troubles. Week after week, he claimed that she was the reason for his failed career, weight problems, and financial woes — he vilified her. I coached him to see that blaming his wife was truly disempowering him. With this blame-filled mind-set, he would have to wait for his *wife* to change before his *life* could change. After I led him through the process outlined below, he discovered that he was actually unhappy with himself and his own actions. He finally realized that only he had the power to change his life, and he began to feel compassion for his wife. He set up an action plan for his career, his health, his finances, and his marriage. Everything changed dramatically for the better when he took his power back. His only regret? That he hadn't stopped playing the blame game sooner!

Challenge: The next time you feel blame, try the following exercise.

1. First, take a deep breath and look at what is causing the blame to bubble up. For example, let's say your coworker dropped the ball and as a result you didn't meet your project deadline. You blame your coworker: how dare he not follow through with his agreement to the team?

2. Next, channel compassion for the person you are blaming. Perhaps your colleague is in the midst of a challenge at home with his teenage son. Take a look at the human being you are blaming, as opposed to the villain you've created.

3. Now, think about empowered solutions. What is the next step toward where you want to go? Perhaps it is time for a heart-to-heart with your coworker about the importance of deadlines and how you feel about falling behind. Maybe you need to talk to your boss about a new checks and balances system that would ensure deadlines are met.

You've now successfully reclaimed your power and created a human connection. (Hint: Make sure to use this process the next time you blame *yourself.*)

Affirmation: Compassion is the key to releasing blame, and I am a wonderfully compassionate person.

"My religion is kindness."

— HIS HOLINESS THE FOURTEENTH DALAI LAMA,
spiritual leader of Tibet and winner of the 1989 Nobel Peace Prize

If I forgive, I condone.

The Truth: Forgiveness is about release. It is an opportunity for you to experience peace. When you forgive, that does not mean you are condoning your own actions or those of another; it simply means you are ready to let go and move forward. Forgiveness is one of the most powerful gifts we can give others and ourselves.

One of the most inspiring stories of forgiveness comes from South Africa and the creation of the Truth and Reconciliation Commission, which allowed victims and perpetrators of the apartheid era to come together to tell their stories in order to create a path to forgiveness. In the words of Archbishop Desmond Tutu, chair of the commission:

> Instead of revenge and retribution, this new nation chose to tread the difficult path of confession, forgiveness, and reconciliation....We were exhilarated as we heard people who had suffered grievously, who by rights should have

been baying for the blood of their tormentors, utter words of forgiveness, reveal an extraordinary willingness to work for reconciliation, demonstrating magnanimity and nobility of spirit....Fundamentally, we are good; we are made for love, for compassion, for caring, for sharing, for peace and reconciliation, for transcendence, for the beautiful, for the true and the good.

We are all capable of forgiving.

Challenge: Take a forgiveness inventory:

- Is there anyone you need to forgive? Honestly assess whether or not you are ready to forgive. If not, ask yourself, "What needs to occur for me to be ready to forgive?" If possible, take action: perhaps you need to write a letter to let your true feelings out (even if this person is no longer living), or maybe you need to call the person and ask for an apology. Perhaps you need to adopt a new perspective about the situation that will allow space for forgiveness. "He was doing the best he could with the information he had" is one perspective that often helps my clients to forgive.

- Is there anything you need to forgive yourself for? Really look deep: perhaps you have been holding on to a mistake you made years ago. Make the decision to forgive yourself. Sometimes it's helpful to write out your mistakes and burn the paper or to take a "forgiveness hike" in which you walk in nature to release your mistakes and forgive.

- Is there anyone you need forgiveness from? Allow this chapter to be a catalyst for you to seek that forgiveness. It is never too late to apologize.

Affirmation: I forgive myself and others with grace and ease.

"We rarely know everything about a situation.
Know all and you will pardon all."
— THOMAS À KEMPIS, German medieval Catholic monk

BIG FAT LIE #42

*If our relationship was meant to be,
sex would be easy.*

The Truth: In the majority of long-term relationships, great sex takes consciousness and effort. I am always amazed that our Inner Critics give us such a hard time about how much (read: how little) sex we are having in monogamous relationships. It is very rare to encounter a long-term monogamous relationship in which sex occurs often and effortlessly. Sure, in the beginning of a new relationship maybe you can't keep your hands off each other, but once the honeymoon period is over it is normal to have ebbs and flows. And it vital that we keep the fire burning so that we experience all the benefits of sex regularly.

Most people I know who are in healthy relationships have built-in date nights (code for making love nights!), and thank goodness they do. It is so important to nourish our sexuality and sensuality. We all deserve to be having great sex — *especially* when we are in monogamous relationships. It's time to give our sexual health the attention it deserves.

150

Challenge: Get in tune with your sexual desires, and express them to your romantic partner. Here are some suggestions to help you get started:

- Make a list of the top ten places you like to be touched and kissed (aside from your genitals). Be creative: Do you love to have your neck nibbled? Your back rubbed? Your feet tickled?
- Write each desire on an index card, then fold each card in half and place it in a bowl. Ask your partner to do the same.
- For the next ten weeks, draw a card from each other's bowl and act on what's written on it for a week. Maybe it is the week of tummy rubs, or maybe head scratches!

Affirmation: The exploration of desire is a lifelong process that makes me feel sensual, vibrant, and alive.

> *"At the touch of love, everyone becomes a poet."*
> — PLATO, ancient Greek philosopher

I can control others.

The Truth: We can only control our own actions. Attempting to control other people is a waste of your energy and will always end in frustration and disappointment. Plus, having a laser focus on someone else merely distracts you from focusing on yourself. That's not to say that we have no impact on others; we inspire and affect others all the time. But when we attempt to *control*, our power to influence melts away.

There is no finer example of the lack of control over others than potty training! When Annabella was two and a half, we began the journey of teaching her how to use the potty. And let me tell you, I was *sure* I could control her in this process. Now, as any parent will tell you, you cannot make your child use the potty. In fact, the more I tried to control Annabella's potty routine, the more she resisted it. The power struggle was intense. Once I finally realized that the Big Fat Lie of control had taken over, I lightened up, and things got much easier. It was only when I truly surrendered, releasing the job of potty training to her, that she took on the job and made it happen. What a lesson in humility!

Challenge: Who do you wish you could control? Identify the people that you (perhaps sometimes secretly) wish would *change* so that you could be happy.

- List the top five people you wish you could control.
- Now, list some positive attributes for each of these people. What do you love and appreciate about them? Do you love your coworker's sense of style? The way your sister-in-law laughs? The great stories your neighbor tells? The independent spirit of your daughter?
- Next, list some ways you could positively influence these people. Do you want to inspire your husband to get healthy? Do you wish you could serve as a beacon of hope for your best friend who is depressed? Bring your focus — and your power — back to yourself.
- Now, before you interact with a person on your "control list," remind yourself of what you love about him or her. Take a moment to remember how you can inspire that person without trying to change him or her.
- Finally, decide to officially surrender all your desires to control this person and situation. Christine Arylo and I teach our students in the Inner Wisdom Circles to open their arms fully into a cross position and shout the following, "I hereby surrender _____ [fill in the person's name and/or situation] to the universe/God/source." We then tell them to let out a sound that signifies release. It might be an "Ahhh" or a loud exhale. Whatever works for you!

You'll discover that the more you focus on what you love about the people on your list, the more you concentrate on your own power, the more you surrender, the more positive you feel about them, and the less you want to control them.

Affirmation: I inspire the best in people.

> *"All our lives we have been trying to get someone else*
> *to change — 'for their own good' — and failing.*
> *Not realizing that by insisting that they change*
> *we were actually preventing them from changing.*
> *And all our lives the secret to their inexplicable resistance*
> *has been hidden in front of our eyes in plain sight:*
> *nothing changes — until we do."*

— AURIELA MCCARTHY, Russian-American author and speaker

If you really loved me, you'd know exactly what I want and need.

Can also show up as:

You should be able to read my mind.

The Truth: Loving someone does not mean that you can read her mind. How on earth can you expect your loved one to know exactly what you want? This is a fairy tale perpetuated by books and movies that present an unrealistic image: the man showing up at the perfect time with the surprise gift that his woman has been secretly yearning for her entire life. Get real! The truth is, when you tell people what you want, you give them the opportunity to honor you. Learning how to communicate your needs and desires is the key to a healthy relationship. Give yourself the gift of being heard and honored.

I have truly awesome parents who always asked me to put together a birthday or holiday wish list. When I was a kid, I spent quite a bit of time putting together this list of items I coveted. It was a magical time to think about what I wanted. When the big day finally arrived and I had the joy of opening presents, I savored every last one and was filled with delight as many of the items on my list appeared before my very eyes. I could tell by the look on my parents' faces that they experienced just as much joy as I did in giving me what I truly wanted.

Why is it, then, that as we grow older we think that expressing exactly what we want cheapens the giving process? That asking for what we need somehow makes the receiving of it less sweet?

Jennifer felt that her partner, Joy, should automatically know when she was upset or overtired and that Joy should certainly just be able to tell when she wanted affirmation. She realized that she was having a lot of silent, embittered conversations inside her head that were poisoning her relationship. Once she decided to give up the mind-reading fantasy, she was able to feel the power of telling the truth about what she wanted and experience the joy of receiving it. Nowadays she'll reach out and call Joy in a moment of chaos and say, "Sweetie, I'm having a horrible day. Can you tell me how wonderful I am, what a great job I'm doing, and how beautiful and lovable I am?" Joy enthusiastically responds with the perfect words at the perfect time because she finally knows exactly what to say to allow Jennifer to feel loved and supported.

Let's declare that it is empowering to ask for what you want and to get it. Step out of the mind-reading trap and into the kind of delight you may have experienced as a kid on your birthday: asking for and getting what you want!

Challenge: In what ways are you hiding your true desires and waiting for someone to read your mind? Fill in the blanks below to find out.

General Relationships

My secret desires that I wish someone would figure out are:

———————————————.

If people really knew me, they'd know that _____
    is really important to me.
    _____ drives me crazy.
    _____ is my secret love.
The thing people often overlook about me is _____.

Mate

I wish my romantic partner would stop _____.
I wish my romantic partner would start _____.
The surprise gift I most yearn for is _____.
I am waiting for my partner to _____.

Work

I wish my boss knew _____ about me.
My biggest unfulfilled needs at work are _____.

Now formulate the preceding information into requests. Now is *not* the time to be coy or subtle, attempting to drop hints and hope someone notices. Get bold in asking for what you want. It may feel awkward at first, but it will become easier and easier...I swear! Start the request with "I have a request. Will you please...?" Be clear and drop the fluff. Here are some sample requests:

- Will you please be on time for our meetings?
- Will you please give me white roses for Valentine's Day this year?
- Will you please stop driving so fast when I'm in the car?
- Will you please give me the Smith account?

You may be met with no, but you could also be met with yes. And when you are met with a yes, recognize and celebrate how good it feels to receive what you truly want and how wonderful it is to see the satisfaction in the giver.

Affirmation: I joyfully ask and gratefully receive.

> *"The thing always happens that you really believe in;*
> *and the belief in a thing makes it happen."*
> — FRANK LLOYD WRIGHT, American architect

I have the power to save/fix another person.

The Truth: We can only influence and inspire others; the saving is up to them. Our Inner Mean Girls like us to believe that if we collude with those we want to save and join them in their depression, sadness, poverty, and/or anger, we will be able to save them. In truth, in order to be a source of inspiration to another person, we need to resist the temptation to join them and instead to shine as brightly as possible and trust they are capable of saving themselves. Sometimes you'll encounter people who are resistant to your inspiration and joy — "energy vampires." They yearn for others to save them and, in the process, suck those around them dry of energy. Stay away from energy vampires and instead focus on your own self-care. You may end up inspiring them to change!

Challenge: Identify the energy vampires in your life. Who do you constantly want to save or fix? Who expects you to save them?

Who leaves you feeling depleted or down? Make a decision either to shift the "saving energy" you carry to "inspiring energy" when you're around this person or to cut her out of your life. Care enough about yourself to put yourself and your best interests first.

Affirmation: I shine brightly so that others may shine…and all this bright light of Truth protects me from the energy vampires of the world.

"I feel with loving compassion the problems of others without getting caught up in their problems that are giving them lessons they need for their growth."

— KEN KEYES, American author and lecturer

*If I just get small enough,
others won't feel bad or jealous.*

Can also show up as:

It's not okay to shine.

The Truth: You're being true to yourself when you allow yourself to shine as brightly as you can, when you let your Inner Superstar out. Those who respond with jealousy or negativity have some work to do on themselves and — quite frankly — that is none of *your* business. Making yourself small will never help others to feel better. You have a responsibility to yourself, and you have full permission to celebrate who you are and to experience the joys of your successes.

Let's explore the reverse for a moment. Call to mind the last time you felt jealous of another, when your Inner Mean Girl made a comparison, making you feel "less than." Notice how this is an indication of the work you need to do. Jealous of your friend's great physique? Underneath the jealousy you'll discover that you're aching to get in better shape. Jealous of your brother's monetary success? Looks like you have some work to do to bring home more dough. This is the truth of jealousy — when you are jealous of another, that signals a hidden desire to create something in your life. This indicates the work you need to do. And when others are jealous of you, trust that it is a sign of the work that *they* need to do.

A note on shining: I have found that our Inner Critics think that in order to shine we must turn into boisterous, larger-than-life jerks. The truth is that when you let your Inner Superstar shine, it is not from an egotistical, self-centered place but rather a soul-filled, radiant place. It feels grounded and real, not inflated and overbearing. This is about you being connected with the truth of your Goddess-given magnificence.

Challenge:

- First, list the situations in which you habitually hide your light under a bushel.
- Notice who surrounds you most frequently in those situations. (Are you at home with your little brother? Are you with that particular coworker who always complains?)
- Note the impact your habit has on those surrounding you. Do you notice them feeling any better? Look deep here. Is your turning down your radiance knob helping others?
- Now list the situations in which you tend to shine bright. (Remember, this is not about being egotistical or larger-than-life. This is about the light within you radiating beautifully outward.)
- Who surrounds you most frequently in those situations? (Are you with your husband? Your Aunt Sally, who loves to hear about your success?)
- Notice the impact on others when you shine bright. Do they celebrate with you? Does your positive energy inspire others?

- What is your particular version of shining? (Is it your quiet smile when you receive a compliment? Is it dancing in the middle of the dance floor to celebrate your accomplishments? Is it shouting, "Yes!" at the top of your lungs on a hike?)
- Great! Finally, commit to shining in one of the situations in which you normally hide your light. Challenge yourself to change this habit, one moment at a time, and notice the impact.

Affirmation: I celebrate, I radiate, I inspire, I shine like the golden sun, and I give others permission to do the same!

> *"Better keep yourself clean and bright.*
> *You are the window through which you must see the world."*
> — GEORGE BERNARD SHAW, Irish playwright
> and cofounder of the London School of Economics

BIG FAT LIES

ABOUT BEING AUTHENTIC

Oscar Wilde put it brilliantly: "Be yourself. Everyone else is already taken." We spend so much time, energy, and money trying to look like, be like, and act like anyone but ourselves... especially when our Inner Critics are in charge. Our Inner Critics and Inner Mean Girls try to protect us at all costs, keeping us from being vulnerable and keeping our hearts tucked away unseen and unknown. They silence us when speaking up isn't easy or popular. Theirs is the voice that whispers, "Be quiet" when the world needs our truth. Our Inner Critics and Inner Mean Girls taught us, when we were very young, that it was easier to fit in and get small than to rock the boat and be genuine.

But your Inner Wisdom knows better. She knows that fully owning who you are and being seen in your Truth is priceless. Truly there is no better feeling than being seen as the original work of art you are. When your Inner Superstar is completely awakened, you can fully express yourself. You'll say to hell with social conventions and the risks of vulnerability and decide to let your "freak flag fly" for all to see. It is delicious to be 100 percent *you*.

So here are the Biggest Fattest Lies that get in the way of you being *you*. Get ready to celebrate the truth of how fabulous you are.

I had better be perfect.

Can also show up as:

It has to be perfect.
I have to get it right.

The Truth: Perfection is unattainable. Let me say that again: perfection is unattainable. Perfection is an absolute that, by mere definition, means there is nothing better out there. When I see clients fall into the trap of perfectionism, I know I need to step in and cry "Stop!" or they'll end up miserable and/or fall into perpetual procrastination. You see, committing to perfection often leads to paralysis; when we fear we may not be doing things "right," we often don't finish tasks or allow ourselves to move forward. Or worse yet, we never even begin things because we have already decided we won't get them right or do them perfectly.

Most people who fall into the trap of perfectionism value excellence and quality but have let that value run amok. In other words, perfectionists take their excellence value way too seriously. They are constantly striving for A+ grades. But guess what? No one is grading you! The universe is not tallying up your score and handing you a report card at the end of the semester. As wildly successful Internet and tele-seminar guru Alex Mandossian says, "Sloppy success is always better than perfect mediocrity."

Susan was a perfectionist in the worst way. Her dogged determination to achieve perfection actually prevented her from starting projects — she was a chronic procrastinator because she was sure that the end product would never be good enough. She lost before she even got started. On the rare occasions that she got over the hump of beginning a project, she couldn't seem to finish it.

Susan came to me because she was fed up with feeling like a failure as a result of this perfectionist cycle. Together, we uncovered her Inner Wisdom's Truth: reaching a finish line was more important to her than being perfect. Susan realized that getting things done would make her feel energetic and confident, so we set up an action plan for completing several outstanding projects. Although at first it was extremely challenging for Susan to move on to the next step in her process when she felt she had completed the last step in a mediocre way, seeing her projects near completion gave Susan courage and strengthened her commitment to value finish lines more than perfection. Today, I'm happy to say, Susan is a recovered perfectionist and remains inspired by the momentum and progress in her life!

Challenge: Take your power back from the beast of perfectionism. Complete the process below:

- What do you get out of being a perfectionist — even if being a perfectionist is just 1 percent of who you are? Do you feel safe? Do you feel like you're always right or in control? Do you avoid presenting your finished projects to the scrutiny of the world?

- What is perfectionism costing you? Are you isolated? Do you spend little time with your loved ones? Are you procrastinating? ("If it can't be perfect, I won't even begin.") Have you lost confidence in your ability to finish tasks?
- What is more important than being perfect? Moving forward and making progress? Being happy? Getting out into the world? Surviving judgment? The rush of connecting with your soul's true purpose?
- Once you've determined what is more important than being perfect, post signs in several places in your home and office to remind yourself. Your sign might read "I value progress more than perfection," "I value joy more than perfection," "I value self-love more than perfection," or "I value my family more than perfection." What will your sign say?

  I value _____ more than perfection.

  Whenever you feel the perfectionist monster heading your way, take a deep breath, look at your sign, and move forward.
- Practice going for the C instead of the A. My dear friend and colleague Samantha Bennett, a recovering perfectionist, invented this tactic when she realized that she got far more done when she let herself off the A+ hook. I know, I know — this will feel like torture to you — but try it anyway. Practice leaving the dirty dishes in the sink before going to bed, put together an outfit that doesn't quite match, or send an email to your friend without proofreading it first. List at least three ways you will give up the A+ and just be a C student this month.
- Notice what happens when you're imperfect or messy — when you go for the C. Did the world end? Did your

friends turn against you? Did your children run in horror? Aha! I didn't think so.

Affirmation: You already created the ideal affirmation for yourself when you wrote "I value _____ more than perfection."

"The 'C' students run the world."

— HARRY S. TRUMAN,
thirty-third president of the United States

They'll hate me if I _____.

Can also show up as:

I need them to like me.
I can please everyone.

The Truth: It's high time we focused on self-approval rather than on the approval of others. Self-approval is paramount to our happiness and is the only type of approval worthy of our pursuit. All too often we put seeking others' approval ahead of liking ourselves. It's time we took a stand to make self-approval the most important kind of approval in our lives.

And believe me when I say that I speak from experience. I know this Big Fat Lie like the back of my hand. I can shrink back and withhold my opinion and needs in order to please people and beef up the illusion that I can make people like and approve of me. I still tense up when I feel like speaking up could result in being disliked, hated, or disapproved of. I have found when I have that sinking feeling, most of the time there is no real risk of my being disliked or disapproved of...it just feels like there is.

Plus, this Lie comes with an underlying flawed premise: we believe we can control other people's feelings toward us. If we think that people will hate us if we do one thing or love us if we do another, this implies that we have control over how much or how little others like us. The truth is that we cannot control how other people feel about us, or about anything else, for that matter. (Be sure to check out Big Fat Lie #43: "I can control others.") I've seen this need to be liked prevent people from putting their art, their great ideas, and their Truth into the world. The fear of rejection and disapproval can become so intense that it can stop people in their tracks.

My client Kathy was launching an art blog. She called in a panic saying, "But, Amy, what if people don't like my paintings? What if the critics slam them?" My response? "Yes, sweetheart, some people won't like them. Some people might even hate them. It's true. And some people will love them. Some people will think your art is genius! And how others feel is none of your business. And utterly out of your control. What is your business? Expressing yourself and bringing to life your unique voice and art." She laughed in relief and decided she needed to get over it. It's time to face the pain of being disliked or disapproved of and to stop letting it get in your way. In some circles they say your first hate mail means you've made it. It means you've stretched beyond your comfort zone and risked. You've cast a wide enough net that it contains both those who love your work and those who hate it. Go on and go big...I dare you!

Challenge: Answer the following questions:

- Where in your life do you find yourself holding out for someone else's approval? Where do you feel as if you are at risk of being disliked and disapproved of? At work? When it comes to your creativity? The project at school?
- What is the fear of rejection and of being disliked costing you? Is it stopping you from putting your art out in the

world? Telling your partner the truth about your political views?

- Shifting the focus back to how much you like you, on a scale of 1 to 10 (1 = total disapproval, 10 = 100 percent approval), how much do you currently approve of yourself and the decisions you've made?
- If the score above is less than a 10, what would 2 points higher look like? If you rated your self-approval at a 6, what would an 8 look like? If you're at a 7, what needs to change for you to get your self-approval to a 9?
- What changes do you need to commit to in order to score a 10?

Congratulations — you've just shifted your power back to yourself and your focus back to self-approval. Bravo!

Affirmation: I approve of me, and I get the last vote every time!

"What you think of me is none of my business."

— TERRY COLE-WHITTAKER,
American author and inspirational speaker

BIG FAT LIE #49

If I become a wife or mother,
I'll lose myself.

The Truth: Human beings are like prisms. Different situations and roles bring out new colors. I remember freaking out when I first became engaged — I thought that if I became a wife I would no longer be me. I worried that I would have to become a different person altogether when I stepped into the role of *wife*; suddenly I would be forced to become society's idea of a wife instead of good ol' Amy. I eventually learned that I get to be *my* version of a wife, not some sitcom version that has been imprinted on my subconscious mind.

I have seen many an expectant mother filled with anxiety over becoming a parent. Mothers can fall into the trap of thinking that they need to change the core of who they are in order to be a good parent. In reality, it is each woman's unique style of parenting that will allow her to be the best parent she can be.

Challenge:

- Grab some blank pieces of paper and some markers. Make a list of all the roles you play: Daughter? Sister? Salesperson? Yoga queen? Artist? CEO?
- Next, take a fresh sheet of paper and divide it up into sections and label each section with one of the various roles you play.
- See if you are playing some roles much more than others. Let those roles take up most of the space on the paper. Get creative and have fun.
- Notice if there are any roles you love to play that are not getting their fair shake. For example, do you love to be the life of the party but haven't socialized in months? Or are you a writer who hasn't written since she became a mom?
- Choose one role that you are neglecting, and commit to embodying that role at least three times within the next month. Maybe the "nature lover" isn't getting enough of your attention. If that's the case, plan to take a hike, schedule a family camping trip, or visit the beach.
- It's time to reclaim *all* of who you are!

Affirmation: I joyfully acknowledge and appreciate every aspect of myself. I express every part of myself with ease.

"Life begins at the end of your comfort zone."

— NEALE DONALD WALSCH,
American author and spiritual messenger

It is more important to be polite than to be authentic.

The Truth: If being polite is getting in the way of being authentically you, it's time to take a deeper look. I'm not talking about common courtesies such as saying "please" and "thank you," for goodness sake — let's celebrate those! I'm talking about how being *you* is sometimes more important than being gracious. I have seen this politeness disease take hold of lives. It seems we've been taught that keeping up appearances is more valuable than being real. It's time to clean up our relationship with courtesy and instead be honest with others and with ourselves about the truth of our lives, even at the risk of appearing rude. After all, how can we experience unconditional love and acceptance if people don't even know who we are?

Mae is a schoolteacher who grew up in a family that valued manners above all else. She was plagued by this later on, constantly torn between politeness and authenticity, and she often felt alone and unseen. Her desire not to contradict anyone, particularly her elders, kept her silent in staff meetings, even though she had some terrific, innovative ideas. She often deferred to her husband to make the decisions in their marriage because she didn't want to step on his toes. Her politeness was inhibiting her personal and professional growth and keeping an invisible wall of separation between her and her husband. In our sessions I helped her open up and show her authentic self to the world. She realized her mask of politeness was preventing her from being 100 percent herself, and after a few months of coaching she began expressing her thoughts and feelings to those she loved in a direct and honest way. In the beginning, she worried that she was being rude but decided to forge ahead and *risk* coming off as impolite in order to be known and heard. She started telling her husband which movie or restaurant she preferred — even before being asked — and she became known at her school as an agent of change. She discovered that the feeling of being deeply witnessed by others was well worth the risk.

Challenge: Discover just how authentic you are by completing the following self-assessment written by fellow life coach and wonderful human being Rich Rusdorf, CPCC.

Authenticity Self-Assessment

Use this questionnaire to get a reading on your current degree of courageous authenticity. Rate yourself from 1 to 5, with 1 being "Describes me" and 5 being "Does not describe me."

1. ____**Engaging courage.** I speak up when facing my fears of abandonment, rejection, ridicule, chastisement, or failure.
2. ____**Being present.** I experience what is in the present moment rather than being preoccupied with the past or future.

3. _____**Being transparent.** I reveal my thoughts, feelings, expectations, judgments, interpretations, and assumptions, letting people know exactly what I am feeling and thinking.

4. _____**Welcoming feedback.** I am openly curious about how others are affected by me.

5. _____**Knowing myself.** I know my strengths, values, life purpose, boundaries, and inner essence.

6. _____**Being spontaneous.** I act and react in the moment, without constraint, reservation, internal judgment, or external force.

7. _____**Embracing the unknown.** I can let go of the need to know how things will turn out.

8. _____**Noticing my intent.** I allow things to happen rather than trying to control or manipulate outcomes.

9. _____**Revising an earlier statement.** I give myself permission to change my mind, to restate an earlier communication, to add clarification, or to clear up a misunderstanding.

10. _____**Holding differences.** I am open to considering viewpoints that are different from mine without feeling that doing so takes something from me.

11. _____**Connecting and reconnecting.** I see the value in everyone and connect with his or her deeper, truer self and essence.

12. _____**Taking back projections.** I take responsibility for my own judgments and interpretations, and focus less on what others do or think.

13. _____**Sharing mixed emotions.** I express the complex feelings of my ambivalence and confusion, and I am comfortable with inconsistencies.

14. _____**Asserting what I want and don't want.** I affirm my right to want what I want, even if it's unreasonable or there is little chance of getting it.

15. ____**Seeing and making choices.** I recognize a variety of perspectives and choose to act in alignment with my values, wants, needs, and best interests.

Score Results

15 to 30: Genuine: You are typically real and sincere.

31 to 45: Pretentious: You are a high-quality image of the real you.

46 to 60: Inauthentic: It's time to stop hiding and let the world know who you are.

I challenge you to be your authentic self by expressing your truth, your opinions, and your feelings, however complex they are. Chose the area above that you rated a 3 or above, and work on that area for the next week. For example, if you scored a 5 on the "revising an earlier statement" skill, work on giving yourself permission to change your mind, to restate an earlier communication, to add clarification, or to clear up a misunderstanding this week.

Affirmation: I am delighted to be 100 percent me.

> *"To love oneself is the beginning of a life-long romance."*
> — OSCAR WILDE, Irish writer and playwright

BIG FAT LIE #51

It's tolerable.

Can also show up as:

It isn't that big a deal.

The Truth: I have a "claim or change" philosophy regarding tolerance. Either consciously *claim* the things/people/circumstances you are tolerating and accept them, or *change* them by taking action: make the decision to hire a trainer and get in shape, officially quit your job, or sell your money-pit of a house.

Let's not kid ourselves: there is a high cost to merely tolerating people or things or circumstances. It diminishes your opinion of yourself and gets in the way of being true to your own needs. Every time you walk by that door that needs fixing or go to a job you loathe or pretend not to notice the way your friend belittles you, you are allowing something that bothers you to take up cherished space in your mind. I always ask my clients to clean up their tolerations so that they create more space for the things they love. They are amazed at how much this process renews their energy and inspiration. It's like doing decluttering and feng shui for your brain. It's time to create more chi in your mind so you

181

can meet the world with zest. Things that you are tolerating can pile up and move from being minor annoyances to being huge wake-up calls. It's time to recognize that you are important and either claim or change each thing you tolerate one by one.

Challenge: What are you currently tolerating? When do you find yourself "putting up with it all"? What are you sick and tired of?

Meditate on this idea for a minute. Look first at the big-picture things you are tolerating: an unhealthy relationship, a home full of clutter, extra body weight, a lousy neighbor. Next, look at the smaller things: an incomplete project, a mediocre paint job, a dirty toilet, clothes that don't fit.

Now, decide whether to claim or change each of these things. Claiming means that you will reframe your perspective. For example, if you've been tolerating a home full of clutter, you could decide to choose and claim your home as a well-lived-in haven for you. Change means that you will take action and transform the circumstances. For example, if you've been tolerating a marriage that is no longer working, you could commit to couples counseling or come to the difficult decision to file divorce papers. Either way, step out of toleration and into empowerment.

Affirmation: I claim my ability to accept and rejoice or to change and take action.

> *"They always say time changes things,*
> *but you actually have to change them yourself."*
>
> — ANDY WARHOL, American painter and filmmaker

*Feeling this way now means
that I always feel this way.*

Can also show up as:

If I let myself feel bad, it will stay.

The Truth: My dear friend Geneva often quips, "I have the worst memory. Whenever I feel down, I think I always feel this way!" The truth is that our moods are always changing — moment by moment, day by day. It's easy to fall into thinking that you always feel upset when you are simply having a bad moment, bad day, or even a bad week.

It can sometimes feel like if we say how we're feeling, it will make the feeling persist. Like somehow lying about how we feel means we won't have to feel that way anymore. In truth, avoidance is what keeps the feelings present. It's been said many times over: what we resist persists. The only way to the other side of your anger, despair, disappointment, grief, jealousy, or fear is through it. You need to feel it, express it, process it, even love it, so it can dissolve.

Which is why the first step in the Wake-Up Call Three-Step

Process is to ask, "What is my Inner Critic/Inner Mean Girl saying?" This question gives you permission to feel the way you are feeling, to tell the truth about how lousy things feel and how mean you are being to yourself, to bring the darkness into the light. But I don't leave you there. We then ask, "What does my Inner Wisdom know?" so you can tap into what you know already on a deep level. And our final step is for you to physicalize your Inner Wisdom's Truth with a gesture, movement, or stance while repeating it aloud.

A teaching in the coaching world goes like this: "What you can't be with runs you." In other words, if you feel like you can never be with anger or sadness or disappointment and therefore spend time and energy avoiding an emotion, then you end up allowing that emotion to be at the center of your life. You are merely dancing around your anger instead of living the richness and fullness of your life. Let's explore how to allow emotions to flow through you so that you can stop avoiding them. And simultaneously you will recognize the impermanence of all your emotions.

Challenge:

- Begin by noticing what emotion you are most scared to feel. Is it anger? Rage? (It is very common for women especially to be afraid of anger, since many of us were raised to believe it was not okay for little girls to get angry or be enraged.) Maybe for you it is sadness or even joy?
- What are you afraid will happen if you allow yourself to feel that emotion? Do you secretly believe you'll end up in a fit of rage and never come out? Get swallowed whole by your sadness? That the other shoe will drop if you feel truly and deeply happy? (See Big Fat Lie #28: If I allow myself to celebrate, the other shoe will drop.)
- What emotion do you believe you always feel when you feel it in the moment? It is all too easy to believe we are

always stressed and on the edge when we're in the midst of being stressed and on the edge!

- The next time you feel any of the emotions you unearthed above bubble to the surface, simply stop and notice it. Notice how you feel in your body. Allow yourself to become fully present with this emotion.
- Simply BE with the feeling. Sit side by side with your anger. Cradle your sadness like a newborn babe. Welcome your feelings of stress and anxiety. And just be.
- What you'll discover is that the less you resist that feeling, the less scary it becomes and the faster it dissipates.

Congratulations, sweet one, you've just practiced mindfulness and unconditional self-love.

Affirmation: The next moment will take care of itself and may bring something completely different — I am willing to be surprised.

> *"This being human is a guest house.*
> *Every morning a new arrival....*
> *Welcome and entertain them all!"*

— RUMI, thirteenth-century Persian poet and Sufi mystic

I'm a good girl. I need to be nice.

Can also show up as:

I can't possibly say that!

The Truth: Shattering the good girl image can be terrifying. And no wonder: we grow up being rewarded over and over for doing what we're told, keeping ourselves in line, and playing nice. But what if that doesn't match up with how we really feel? What if we are screaming "NO MORE!" underneath all the niceties? How about trying on "Why, yes, this is a big deal, thank you very much"? What if the only way to feel true to who you *really* are is to drop the nice girl act and say how you really feel? LOUDLY.

Betsy was an administrative assistant in an unhappy marriage, and over the years she had placated her feelings so often that she didn't even know how she felt anymore. When I first asked her, "What do you want?" she stared at me as though I had two heads. She had absolutely no idea of how to answer any question about her opinions or feelings. She had spent so long catering to the needs of her husband and her boss that she had forgotten how to even ask herself what *she* wanted. She was plagued by the syndrome of

186

being nice, being the good girl, constantly putting her own feelings and needs on the back burner. And her body was started to be affected as well (read: constant health issues). I could see that if she didn't stop being so nice, she would become really ill, really soon. We began by doing the exercise below, and Betsy learned how to stand up for herself at work — no more staying late just because her boss was having an anxiety attack — and at home, letting her husband fend for himself one night a week while she went out with her friends from church. As Betsy increasingly surrounded herself with people who loved her for herself alone and not just because she was so compliant, she felt better, she ate better, and she even started going for long walks during her lunch hour. Her mental, spiritual, and physical health all improved. And she loved it when I asked her the question, "What do *you* want?"

Challenge: Let's get you out of the superficial land of nice and into the land of being you by pushing the boundaries of how you're perceived.

- To begin, I want you to explore what holds you in the "good girl" headlock by looking at what you are scared of. What is the worst name someone could call you? Is it bitch? Diva? High maintenance? Really pick the label that gets your blood pumping and brings out your fear. For example, you might say, "I am terrified of being perceived as a bitch; therefore I continue to play the good girl game at all costs."
- Next, assess what the good girl label has been costing you. Do you always pick up everyone else's slack and never have any time for you? Are you staying in a relationship that doesn't work anymore because you fear he'll call you a bitch? Do you end up pretending things don't bother you that are really eating you alive because you don't want to be perceived as high maintenance? Be real and honest with yourself here.

- Try on the label that most scares you for a day. Notice how liberating it can feel to be what you're most afraid of. Allow yourself to explore your version of being a bitch for a day: "I can't pick up your kids and keep them for three hours while you go get a massage today." Be high maintenance: "I would like the dressing on the side and whole wheat toasted lightly, thank you very much." Explore your inner diva: "Actually, I don't like it when you assume I'll go with you. I'm booked."
- Notice the impact. What I know to be true is that if you've been being the nice girl for the past five decades, your version of being a bitch will likely be the world's version of being assertive. Your version of being a diva is likely most people's version of simply requesting what they need.
- Deepen the learning. What did you learn, and what are you willing to incorporate into your daily life? Get specific about what felt authentic and more in line with who you really are.
- Finally, write yourself a permission slip, and put it somewhere special. On the permission slip, list out specific ways you'll allow yourself to drop the nice girl and good girl act and live a more authentic life.

Affirmation: I'm willing to risk being perceived as a _____ [fill in the blank with your feared label from above] in order to find my voice.

> *"Honesty and frankness make you vulnerable.*
> *Be honest and frank anyway."*
>
> — KENT M. KEITH, author and speaker

BIG FAT
LIES
ABOUT
YOUR
SPIRIT

There are big questions in life, questions that go beyond our everyday thinking, leading us to wonder who we really are, why we're here, how we can stay connected to our spirit, and more. The challenge arises when we let our Inner Critics take over our spiritual questioning, sending us down a rabbit hole of chaos, leading to more disconnection and stress. Add to that natural disasters, inexplicable illnesses in good people we love (or even ourselves), and we can end up feeling depressed and hopeless, as though there is no higher power to speak of and that we're in this alone. It's no wonder it can feel easier to distract ourselves with everything from reality TV to food to drugs to constant shopping. Why try to be present when the present is so hard to be with?

A true solution? Turning to your Inner Wisdom and nourishing your spirit, which creates a respite from this avalanche of despair. Having and keeping a daily spiritual practice is key to being the calm in the center of the storm. It gives you a strong foundation of self-love and inner peace and is the best way out of the madness. So let's take a Lie-by-Lie look at what keeps us from our inner state of calm and tap into the Truth. Take a deep breath, relax your shoulders, and get ready to deepen your connection to your higher power, higher self, the universe, God, Spirit, the Divine, source energy, nature — whatever you call that feeling of being plugged in.

BIG FAT LIE #54

I don't need a spiritual practice.

The Truth: Honey, we all need a spiritual practice...especially in today's fast-paced, chaotic world. The trick is to find a practice that works for you, one that feeds your soul, fuels your spirit, and fills you with delight.

I've coached thousands of clients from all kinds of religious backgrounds: Catholic, Christian, Jewish, Hindu, Buddhist, Wiccan, agnostic, atheist, and more. And I can tell you from experience that the happiest and healthiest Inner-Superstar-shining-bright people have a daily practice. They have found something that connects them to themselves and their spirit every day. Whether is it praying, meditating, dancing, walking in nature, or playing the drums LOUD, they are doing it regularly in order to free themselves of their Inner Critics and to become fully present to their own hearts and magnificence. It's not about finding the time; it's about creating and claiming the space for you to cherish *you*.

You need to view the time you spend doing your practice as a gift to yourself, not as an obligation or burden. It's time to stop making excuses about why you're not doing it and begin today.

Challenge: Let's create a daily practice that will feel absolutely divine and delicious:

- Begin by thinking about what fuels you. Do you love music? Is nature your church? Is silence a cherished rarity in your life? Are you crazy about dancing? Decide on one joyful, nourishing ritual to do for a daily practice experiment.
- Next, decide on the time of day that is the most sacred for you. I recommend morning time, but being a busy working mom myself, I know that mornings can be total chaos and it could be easy to miss your appointed time. Use whatever time of day works for you, and slot your practice in between two established habits. In other words, tether your daily practice to something you can count on yourself for. For example, you could sandwich your practice between brushing your teeth and drinking your cup of coffee or tea. Or put it between putting your kids to bed and watching TV.
- Set a timer for your practice experiment. Using a timer will give your practice a beginning, middle, and perhaps most important of all, an end. If you're starting from scratch, begin with only a three-minute commitment. Work your way up to fifteen or twenty minutes throughout the next few months. Remember, your practice, which can be anything from breathing deep to listening to your favorite song to standing outside barefoot in the grass — whatever feels right — is going to be fun and nurturing.

- Go easy on yourself! Allow this new habit to be fun. Take bold baby steps to create your new habit.
- Notice how you feel when you gift yourself with a daily practice. Do you feel more centered? Less stressed? More present?

Sometimes it can take time for your daily practice to have a powerful positive effect. When I first started my daily meditation practice, on some days I would sit and breathe and watch in horror as anxiety bubbled up as I obsessed over my to-do list for fifteen minutes. Not exactly what I had in mind! But I kept with it, and now I feel so blessed to do my practice. It gets me completely present so I feel alive and plugged into my life.

Want more juicy ideas? Christine Arylo and I created a wonderful eBook called *Super Power Your Day: Daily Practices for the 21st Century Woman* that you will receive for free in the reader's tool kit at www.BigFatLiesTheBook.com.

Affirmation: I joyfully pause, meditate, and visualize each day. It is my habit, and it is sooo easy.

> *"Let us be silent,*
> *that we may hear the whispers of the gods."*

— RALPH WALDO EMERSON, American philosopher and poet, leader of the Transcendentalist movement

I have to suffer in order to grow.

The Truth: Suffering is a part of life. But that does not mean we need to self-sabotage by creating painful circumstances in order to grow or have a spiritual experience. Joy is just as deep an emotion as — if not deeper than — pain and suffering. It is more than possible to be joyful and to grow at the same time, deepening your connection to source. Likewise, art can be created from places of deep joy. Need some evidence? Pick up a copy of Pablo Neruda's love poems or Rumi's mystical poetry to experience the brilliance that can grow out of deep bliss.

I've seen how easy it is to become addicted to suffering, especially for those who grew up in a family that felt suffering and sacrifice was the only pathway to God. Take Betty, who grew up in a strict Irish Catholic family where food was scarce and church was required. She was taught that suffering was the key to the kingdom of heaven. At a young age she was taught that anything that felt good, such as listening to music, spending hours talking to her girlfriends about boys, or getting a special dress for a school dance were the "devil's playground." So Betty spent her life creating suffering, scarcity, and rigidity. No concerts, no idle girlfriend chat, and certainly no new dresses. And she couldn't figure out why it felt so right and virtuous to suffer. Together we uncovered how she had unconsciously defined suffering as virtuous and devout. We learned that she felt closer to God when she was tormented, sad, or depressed. And she felt disconnected from Spirit, and even ashamed, when thing were going well. Suffering had become Betty's spiritual "crack pipe." She felt like she needed the drama and chaos of suffering to create deep meaning and growth in her life and thus feel close to the Divine. Things would begin to go well, and Betty would find herself jonesing for a hit of suffering or pain to feel connected. Betty was finally ready to step out of this trap and create joy as a way into spiritual connection.

Betty began to collect evidence of how she also felt the presence of source energy during the happiest moments of her life, such as falling in love, birthing her children, and singing her heart out. She began to accept joy and happiness as teachers of the deeper things in life. And, bit by bit, she released her addiction to pain and suffering. She instilled and nurtured in herself and her children the belief that joy is the kingdom of heaven. Betty chose to believe that God wants us to be happy and that her own joyful expression was a testimony to Spirit. In our last session together, Betty presented me with a link to a video of her joyfully singing a solo with the Praise Band at her church — and she looked beautiful in her brand-new dress.

Challenge: Uncover Lies you may be telling yourself about pain and joy by answering the following questions:

- What does pain mean to you?
- What gift does pain bring you?
- What virtues are reveled when you suffer?

- What does joy mean to you?
- What are your deepest experiences of joy to date?
- How can you further correlate joyful and abundant times with spiritual connection?

Affirmation: I accept joy as my teacher. Happiness is deeply meaningful. God wants me to be happy.

> *"People have a hard time letting go of their suffering.*
> *Out of a fear of the unknown,*
> *they prefer suffering that is familiar."*

— THICH NHAT HANH,
Vietnamese-French Buddhist monk and author

BIG FAT LIE #56

I have no purpose in life.

The Truth: All of us have a purpose, and all of our lives have meaning. It is time for you to realize your life's unique purpose — to rejoice in the things that make you feel passionate, vibrant, and alive.

Whenever I read any of Dr. Seuss's books to my daughter, I am always struck by how beautifully he illustrates that each one of us has a unique purpose: "Today you are you! That is truer than true! There is no one alive who is you-er than you!" I love knowing that kids around the world are receiving these messages about being fully themselves and understanding their unique purpose in the world. Let this chapter connect you to this powerful message.

I know it can be incredibly painful to feel disconnected from and mystified by your life purpose. So many clients come to coaching to get support for uncovering what they are on this planet to do. Below I offer the best exercises I know for putting you on the path to your highest calling.

Challenge: Our quest is for you to uncover and truly plug into your life's purpose, your highest calling. Even if you feel you already have a clearly defined life's purpose, pick at least two of the exercises below as must-do assignments. And as your understanding of your life's purpose deepens, feel free to revisit these exercises. Sometimes revising or adding to your statement of purpose can be a wonderful tonic!

- *Call in your purpose:* First, I want you to set the clear intention that you're ready to fully claim your highest calling. Let the Divine know that you are inviting clarity about your life purpose. Say aloud an invocation, prayer, or intention: "Dear universe, I am ready to receive clarity about my life purpose. I welcome, and vow to pay attention to, your signs and signals."
- *Visualize:* Next try the following visualizations to tap into your purpose:
  1. Imagine that you're in your nineties, sitting in a rocking chair on your front porch, when a small child comes up to you and says, "What was your life for?" How do you answer?
  2. If you had the chance to design a billboard that stood over a highway in a major city, what would it look like? What would your billboard say? Would you use words? Only pictures? What colors are dominant? What is the intention behind your message?
- *Receive feedback:* Ask three people who know you very well what they see as your life purpose or highest calling. Receive the feedback. Really receive it. Sometimes an outsider has wonderful perspectives to offer about our impact.

- *Ask for guidance:* Take out a piece of paper and put the question, "What is my life purpose?" on top of the page, and then let your Inner Wisdom write the answer. Do stream-of-consciousness writing...no censoring...let it flow. Invite in spirit to speak through you. You can also write this question on a piece of paper before going to bed and allow your answers to come to you in your dreams. After your night of sleep, before speaking, write down your dreams and see what messages they reveal.
- *Create your life purpose statement:* Notice the overlap of your visualizations, feedback from outsiders, and your journaling. See if you can come up with a life purpose statement. It could be as simple as "I'm a wake-up call" or "I am here to mother Jack and Sam and be a beacon of hope for my community." Allow yourself to have a working life purpose statement. It doesn't need to be perfect!

Affirmation: I am grateful that I'm living my highest calling.

*"There is vitality, a life-force, an energy,
a quickening that is translated through you into action
and because there is only one of you in all of time,
this expression is unique. And if you block it,
it will never exist through any other medium and be lost."*

— MARTHA GRAHAM, American dancer, choreographer,
and pioneer of modern dance

I should be over this loss by now.

Can also show up as:

There is one right way to grieve.

The Truth: Mourning and grieving are extremely personal processes, and we all have our own ways to go about them. When I initially wrote this chapter, I had just experienced the unexpected, tragic loss of my beloved mother-in-law, Johnnie. (Yes, she was a woman with a man's name, and that was far from the most unique thing about her — she was one of a kind!) Right after her death my husband said to me, "I feel like I'm grieving wrong." And I had thoughts such as, "How on earth do I have the right to experience any joy right now in the face of her death?" and "When will I be over this?" It became clear to me that there are many, many Big Fat Lies about grief swirling around.

Grieving is a process to be taken moment by moment, breath by breath, step-by-step. I speak from experience when I tell you that there is no right way to grieve and that it is more than okay to experience joy while grieving. In some ways, *living* is one of the most powerful ways we can celebrate the life of a person who has passed on.

It's been well over five years since my mother-in-law passed, and waves of grief still wash over me — sometimes at the most unexpected times, such as when the laugh of a stranger in the supermarket reminds me of her or when my daughter does something extra cute and I realize that Johnnie and Annabella will never meet. Instead of thinking that there will be a time when I am over this loss, I've come to accept my grief and have integrated it into my life, with an understanding that "getting over it" is not the goal.

Challenge: Uncover your feelings about grief by looking at the following questions:

- Think about the last time you experienced grief. How did you express it?
- How did others who were mourning express their grief?
- Notice the differences and the range of expressions. (Perhaps you noticed in yourself or others an increase in drinking, sleeping, working, eating, cheerleading, crying, seeking alone time, and so on.)
- Was there a point when people expected you to be over the loss?
- Did you carry expectations about the appropriateness of grieving in certain ways or at certain times?
- What did you feel was the "right" way to grieve?
- Finally, acknowledge your beliefs and expectations about mourning. The next time you are faced with a loss of a loved one, allow yourself to experience grief without judgment.

Affirmation: I celebrate being alive for myself and on behalf of my loved ones who have passed on.

*"Those who will not slip beneath the still surface of the well
of grief, turning downward through its black water
to the place we cannot breathe, will never know the source
from which we drink, the secret water, cold and clear,
nor find in the darkness glimmering the small round coins
thrown away by those who wished for something else."*

— DAVID WHYTE, Irish poet

> *There must be
> something more than this.*
>
> Can also show up as:
>
> *Someday my life will begin.*

The Truth: This is it. This is life. There are times when life feels exhilarating and passionate and times when it feels boring, static, or depressing. You, and only you, get to decide the perspective that you live from at any given moment.

Maybe you've hit an existential crisis on a banner birthday ending with a 0 (midlife, anyone?). Or perhaps you feel you've crashed into yet another roadblock in your career and you feel a sense of hopelessness that it will never change. Maybe you just achieved a major goal that took years to accomplish and you realized winning was not all it was cracked up to be. It's as if your Inner Critic is watching you chase your own tail, shouting into a megaphone the ominous question, "Is this all there is?" as you feel the sweat starting to drip down your brow.

The truth is that this moment, right now, is your life…the good, the bad, and the ugly. If you have a deep sense of dissatisfaction, please do create some bold changes that are in line with your life purpose. Be cautioned, though, that your Inner Mean Girl will be itching to be put in charge when this Lie is present. Your Inner Critic might decide you need to do a complete life makeover and quit everything and move to Paris, when what you really need is a simple perspective shift!

So, with the exercise below, let's look at creating a perspective shift about the wonder and joyousness of your life right now. After all, your life begins at birth (you coming from home) and ends with death (you returning to home), and the time in between is your time for exploration and adventure. I recommend that you have as much fun as you can along the way, knowing that at each moment you have an opportunity to enjoy the bliss, feel the intensity, and revel in the joy of being alive. Breathe deep, dear one, and drink it in! This is it — the real deal. So why not enjoy the ride?

Challenge: Here is an exercise loosely inspired by the brilliant choreographer Bill T. Jones and his work *Still/Here*. (You can learn more about *Still/Here* in the Bill Moyers documentary by the same name, available at shopPBS.org.)

Let's begin with some creative fun:

- Get out a piece of paper, and, working swiftly, draw a "treasure map" of your life.
- Where on the page did you start? The middle? The edge? What color is that part of the map? What shape is it? And what was the path to the next stopping point? And the next?
- Feel free to add words or images if you like. You can represent your journey and your stopping places however you like. Are there some jagged lines to convey your frenetic energy as a young person? Is the starting place a circle with a heavy outline to communicate the solid wall around your family unit? Is there a place on the map

where you just go around and around in crazy circles? (There certainly is on mine — I think it was called my twenties!)

- There's no right or wrong way to do this. It's meant to be purely impressionistic — and no one need ever see it but you — so don't worry about making it perfect, just make it spontaneous!

Now that you have this visual representation of your life, reflect on your journey so far:

- Where are you on your path? Still near the beginning? In the middle of the middle?
- Where would you like this map to go next?
- How would you draw the next portion of your life?
- And how can you commit to enjoying your life? It may be a treasure hunt, but you yourself are the real treasure.

Affirmation: My life is a delicious treasure hunt, and I am the treasure!

"Life is supposed to be fun."

— ESTHER AND JERRY HICKS,
American authors and spiritual teachers

Only near-death experiences serve as wake-up calls.

The Truth: You can claim your own wake-up call. I invite you to right now — in this very moment, allow this chapter to be your very own wake-up call. Don't believe that the only way you'll ever feel truly alive is when you're faced with death or are reminded that time is short. Instead, I want you to choose to live life to the fullest each day.

I have a dear friend who was in a terrible car accident years ago. She had a near-death experience — she saw the white light that many people speak of and heard an omnificent voice that gave her clear direction on what her life purpose was. Wow! Talk about an amazing experience. It made me wonder if there was some way to have that sort of clarifying wake-up call experience, minus the car accident and near-death experience. So I experimented with myself (and my clients) and found that we can tap into that sort of wake-up call experience and connect with our higher self any time we choose. Let me show you how.

Challenge: Take yourself through the process below:

- Drop whatever you are doing for a moment and check in. Close your eyes and focus on your breath. Breathe in and out *slowly* five times. Really get in tune with yourself.
- Notice how your body feels. Are you tense in your shoulders? Queasy in your stomach? Buzzing in your feet? Do a full body scan to become even more present. Allow all tension to fade away, feeling a golden light shining down on you, and take another breath.
- Next, take a priority inventory. What do you view as your number one priority? Is it family? Friends? Career? Health? What *really* matters to you?
- Do a time comparison. How much time are you devoting to your number one priority? If family is number one and you spend only 10 percent of your time with them, something is out of whack! If your health is most important but you regularly skip workouts and stay late at the office, things have got to change.
- Do a death check-in. It may sound morbid, but it is vital to ask: If you knew you had only one year left to live, how would you spend your time? Would you finally travel to Europe? Would you get out of that unhealthy relationship? Would you stop being cruel to yourself and start practicing unconditional self-love?
- Stop putting things off. What have you been putting off? Where in your life have you "gone to sleep"?
- Make a bold change. If you notice that your priorities and time are disconnected, now is the time to make a change. If you realize that you would quit everything and start anew if you had one year left to live, now is the time to get radical. If you have been putting off things that are important to you, now is the time to be bold and act.

• Commit. Commit to making three radical changes in your life. Share your commitment with at least one account-ability partner.

Affirmation: I am alive, awake, and aware of my life each moment.

*"Why wait for a near-death experience
when life itself is a near-death experience?"*

— BONNIE FRIEDMAN, American writer

Afterword: Your Inner Superstar Awakened

Good morning! No matter what time of day it is as you are reading this, I welcome you to the dawning of a new day, a new beginning. Simply the act of recognizing your negative thoughts as Big Fat Lies is a revelation. It means that you've tapped into the truth about who you really are: a magnificent, fabulous, amazing woman with so much to offer the world and herself. You are a Superstar shining bright!

You've begun the journey of fully awakening your Inner Superstar. And this process will continue for the rest of your life. With each new day, new desire, new challenge, and new circumstance you have an opportunity to dive into the well of your Inner Wisdom's Truth and let your Inner Superstar shine. I encourage you day by day, moment by moment, to go back to how you feel. Any time you are feeling a painful emotion, that is a warning sign that you are in the presence of a Big Fat Lie and that you're falling under the spell of your Inner Mean Girl. So take a moment and review the three-step process.

The Wake-Up Call Three-Step Process

- *Step One:* Ask yourself, "What is my Inner Mean Girl/ Inner Critic saying?" Give voice to the Big Fat Lies you are swallowing. Bring them out of the darkness and into the light so they can be healed. Don't hold back here… rant! Let it out!

- *Step Two:* Close your eyes, take a deep breath, and ask yourself, "What does my Inner Wisdom know?" Sink into the land of your Inner Wisdom's Truth. This is the place that feels grounded. It feels like *home.* Really let the Truth wash over you and disintegrate the Big Fat Lies. Ahhh…that feels better! (Remember that even if your Inner Wisdom is delivering a hard, tough-love Truth, it will feel so much better than when your Inner Critic berates you with it. Your Inner Wisdom comes from a compassionate, loving place, whereas your Inner Mean Girl's Lies come from shame and guilt.)

- *Step Three:* Lock in your Inner Wisdom's Truth by repeating it back (aloud if possible) with a physical gesture to tap it in. My Inner Wisdom has me lightly touch my heart; I have a client who waves her hand and another who touches her belly. This will become your touchstone for stepping into Truth and feeling better. It will allow you to lay down a new neural pathway in your brain that serves as a shortcut to your Truth. My clients and I can now simply do that physical gesture anytime we feel the Lies coming on and immediately feel relief and connection to our Inner Wisdom's Truth.

As you practice this process, you will feel your Inner Superstar radiating her strength and power more often, until you at last feel that she is present almost all the time.

I encourage you to revisit this book every few months to see if a new Big Fat Lie has cropped up. Then do the coaching challenge and step into your Truth. I'd love to support you, and I invite you to join my online community and to have access to thousands of dollars' worth of tools in my reader's tool kit as my thank you for joining me on this journey. Join us at www.BigFatLiesTheBook .com. We'd love to have you share your stories of breaking free, of challenge, and of growth.

Even though I've been coaching for many, many years and teaching how to break free of negative self-talk and Inner Critics, I still have moments where my Inner Mean Girl's Lies get the best of me, especially when I step up to the next level and take risks and play big. It is painful and embarrassing and frustrating. But it is *human* to have these voices come up. This book provides you with tools that you will use for the rest of your life. At no time can we simply check off the box and say, "I'm officially over negative self-talk." Instead we continue to use our tools, to grow, and to practice self-compassion and self-love.

Keep finding the love and compassion, and *trust* that the tools are here for you and that you will come into mastery. May you bask in the glow of your power and light. Shine bright!

With unstoppable enthusiasm and great love,

Amy

Acknowledgments

This book was first conceived way back in 2005, and it has taken many years of inspiration, work, and love to birth this baby. Many friends, family members, loved ones, clients, and colleagues contributed to this long-awaited birthday! I owe so much to so many people...

First and foremost, I want to thank my brilliant dear friend, colleague, and soul sister, Samantha Bennett, who has been with me since the beginning, when we had many writing dates over coffee and panini in a Los Feliz coffee shop. I am filled with gratitude for your dazzling edits and feedback, accountability, support, and belief in me and this book. Sam, you are a genius, and I love you so.

After finishing my first draft in 2006, I handed it off to my first two official readers, the remarkable Melanie Abrams and Michele Colgan, and later to more generous readers, including Rob Ahlers, Maria McCann, Russ and Linda Grant, Eddie Conner, Rachel Ashton, Melissa McFarlane, Dyana Valentine, Kristiina Hiukka, Mary Colgan, Matt Genson, and Nadine Risha, all of whom spent hours reading and inspiring me to give more with their phenomenal feedback about my book, book cover, and book proposal. Katie Baker then took all that feedback and created an incredible book edit a few years ago. Thank you ALL so very much!

My family has supported me tirelessly throughout this adventure, especially my husband, Rob; my daughter, Annabella; my mom and dad, Linda and Russ Grant; my big sister, Laura Palmer, and her husband and kids — Todd, Max, Ellie, and Sam; my little "sister," Becky Cusack, and her husband and kids — Brian, Brody, Adam, and Aubrey; and all my cousins, aunts, uncles, and relatives near and far. I feel so blessed to have a family that loves and supports me unconditionally — I hit the jackpot with this family!

I am oh-so-grateful for my incredible support systems, including my Mindful Mamas group, whose members always remind me to be in the moment and fill me up with love: thank you Alison Pennington, Kelley Callahan, Nicole George, Stacey Seifert, Susan McGrath, and Teresa Kaplan; for those in my Femmamind Circle who believe in me and have given me so much support in so many ways: thank you Carol Allen, Christine Arylo, Kristine Carlson, Kami Gray, and Karen Russo; for my Friday Divas, Dyana Valentine and Samantha Bennett: you ladies inspire me so; for Tarja Stoeckl and Ariana Pritchett: thank you for being supportive goddesses in every way possible.

I have incredible appreciation for all the luminaries and teachers who have inspired and supported me with their encouragement, advice, love, and more: especially the geniuses, Claire Zammit, Mike Robbins, Steve Sisgold, Lissa Rankin, Marci Shimoff, Lisa Nichols, Chris Kyle, Chellie Campbell (special gratitude for introducing me to your agent!), Shiloh Sophia McCloud, Kate Winch, and Bob Hessler and his gift of wisdom and mentorship. Thank you to Esther and Jerry Hicks and the Teachings of Abraham, which I first encountered in 1999, and which has greatly influenced my life and my work in more ways than I even know. Thank you to the Coaches Training Institute (CTI) and the Bigger Game Company for their remarkable training. Thank you to all my mentors, partners, and coaches along the way, especially Melissa McFarlane, who inspired me to become a coach way back in 2000 and was my business partner for more than seven years — I've learned so much from you. To Linda Sivertsen, the book proposal coach filled with love and light, thank you for your words and advice and for pushing me to dig deep. Thank you to my agent, Lisa Hagan, and to my PR guardian angel, Jill Daniel.

For Christine Arylo, my partner at Inner Mean Girl Reform School and the Inner Wisdom Circles, thank you for your incredible support and love and for being such a teacher to me on so many levels. You are a queen, and I love you! Huge thanks go to SARK (Susan Ariel Rainbow Kennedy), who first inspired me through her books and now inspires me through her friendship and mentorship. Thank you for the introduction to New World Library, thank you for the walks on the beach, thank you for the miracles and angels, thank you for writing the foreword. It is so juicy and delicious to have the privilege to call you friend.

And finally, I thank the team at New World Library, especially Kim Corbin and my editor Georgia Hughes. Thank you for all your hand-holding through this incredible process. Your edits, your energy, and your hard work are so appreciated.

Notes

A *ll websites accessed June 10, 2011.*

Introduction

Page 2 *"By many objective measures the lives of women in the United States..."* Betsey Stevenson and Justin Wolfers, "The Paradox of Declining Female Happiness." Available at www.nber.org/papers/w14969.

Page 4 *"Despite having written five books,..."* Elizabeth Gilbert, "The Key to a Well-Lived Life: Lighten Up!" Available at http://www.oprah.com/spirit/Elizabeth-Gilbert-on-Failure-and-Living-Well.

Page 4 *"I'm mad at myself...."* Oprah Winfrey, "How Did I Let This Happen Again?" Available at http://www.oprah.com/spirit/Oprahs-Battle-with-Weight-Gain-O-January-2009-Cover/1.

Big Fat Lie #19:
I have no control over my body and my health.

Page 74 *"The term 'stress,' as it is currently used,..."* American Institute of Stress, "Stress, Definition of Stress, Stressor, What Is Stress?, Eustress?" Available at http://www.stress.org/topic-definition-stress.htm.

Big Fat Lie #41: If I forgive, I condone.

Page 147 *"Instead of revenge and retribution…"* Desmond Tutu, "Let South Africa Show the World How to Forgive." Available at http://www.sol.com.au/kor/19_03.htm.

Big Fat Lie #56: I have no purpose in life.

Page 198 *"Today you are you!"* Dr. Seuss, *Happy Birthday to You!* (New York: Random House, 1959).

Resources

Books

Ask and It Is Given: Learning to Manifest Your Desires by Esther and Jerry Hicks

Be Yourself, Everyone Else Is Already Taken: Transform Your Life with the Power of Authenticity by Mike Robbins

By the Way, You Look Really Great Today by Samantha Bennett

Calling in "The One": 7 Weeks to Attract the Love of Your Life by Katherine Woodward Thomas

Choosing Me before We: Every Woman's Guide to Life and Love by Christine Arylo

Don't Sweat the Small Stuff for Women: Simple and Practical Ways to Do What Matters Most and Find Time for You by Kristine Carlson

Emotional Freedom: Liberate Yourself from Negative Emotions and Transform Your Life by Judith Orloff

The Female Brain by Louann Brizendine

The Game of Life and How to Play It by Florence Scovel Shin

Glad No Matter What: Transforming Loss and Change into Gift and Opportunity by SARK

Happy for No Reason: 7 Steps to Being Happy from the Inside Out by Marci Shimoff

Heal Your Mind, Rewire Your Brain by Patt Lind-Kyle

The Hidden Messages in Water by Masaru Emoto

Kicking the Big But Syndrome by Eddie Conner

Loving What Is: Four Questions That Can Change Your Life by Byron Katie

The Money Keys: Unlocking Peace, Freedom & Real Financial Power by Karen Russo

The Soulmate Secret by Arielle Ford

Succulent Wild Woman by SARK

Taming your Gremlin: A Surprisingly Simple Method for Getting Out of Your Own Way by Rick Carson

The Wealthy Spirit: Daily Affirmations for Financial Stress Reduction by Chellie Campbell

What's Your Body Telling You?: Listening to Your Body's Signals to Stop Anxiety, Erase Self-Doubt and Achieve True Wellness by Steve Sisgold

What's Up Down There?: Questions You'd Only Ask Your Gynecologist If She Was Your Best Friend by Lissa Rankin

A Woman's Worth by Marianne Williamson

Websites

DyanaValentine.com: Dyana Valentine's coaching work.

FemininePower.com: Feminine power.

InnerMeanGirl.com: Inner Mean Girl Reform School.

LoveIsIntheStars.com: Carol Allen's wonderful relationship work.

Masaru-Emoto.net: Masura Emoto's website, with water crystal pictures.

NadineRisha.com: Nadine Risha's phenomenal music and meditation tracks.

TheOrganizedArtistCompany.com: Samantha Bennett's The Organized Artist Company.

About the Author

A my Ahlers, the Wake-Up Call Coach, is on a mission to wake up your Inner Superstar so you shine bright. She is a celebrated certified Coach, the CEO of Wake-Up Call Coaching (www.WakeUpCallCoaching.com), the cocreator of Inner Mean Girl Reform School (www.InnerMeanGirl.com), and the innovator of many tele-seminars such as Women Masters and New Man, New Woman, New Life, where she has spoken alongside luminaries such as Marianne Williamson, Neale Donald Walsch, Barbara Marx Hubbard, SARK, Lisa Nichols, Marci Shimoff, Peggy McColl, and many, many more.

Amy has been a featured expert for ABC TV, the *Washington Post*, the *Huffington Post*, the *Oakland Tribune*, and many radio shows. She received the 2011 Women Who Dare award from Girls Inc. for her work with women in the field of health and wellness, and she leads workshops to inspire women to stop being hard on themselves and to wake up to their true magnificence. Amy resides in the San Francisco Bay Area with her beloved husband, Rob, their sweet pea of a daughter, Annabella, and their relentlessly energetic mutt, Dozer.

NEW WORLD LIBRARY is dedicated to publishing books and other media that inspire and challenge us to improve the quality of our lives and the world.

We are a socially and environmentally aware company, and we strive to embody the ideals presented in our publications. We recognize that we have an ethical responsibility to our customers, our staff members, and our planet.

We serve our customers by creating the finest publications possible on personal growth, creativity, spirituality, wellness, and other areas of emerging importance. We serve New World Library employees with generous benefits, significant profit sharing, and constant encouragement to pursue their most expansive dreams.

As a member of the Green Press Initiative, we print an increasing number of books with soy-based ink on 100 percent postconsumer-waste recycled paper. Also, we power our offices with solar energy and contribute to nonprofit organizations working to make the world a better place for us all.

Our products are available
in bookstores everywhere.
For our catalog, please contact:

New World Library
14 Pamaron Way
Novato, California 94949

Phone: 415-884-2100 or 800-972-6657
Catalog requests: Ext. 50
Orders: Ext. 52
Fax: 415-884-2199
Email: escort@newworldlibrary.com

To subscribe to our electronic newsletter, visit
www.newworldlibrary.com

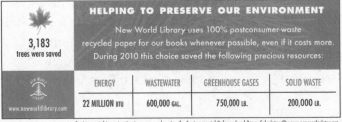